W9-CZT-560

Between Slavery and Freedom

BLACKS IN THE DIASPORA

Darlene Clark Hine, John McCluskey, Jr., and David Barry Gaspar
General Editors

Between Slavery and Freedom

Philosophy and American Slavery

Howard McGary and Bill E. Lawson

Indiana University Press

BLOOMINGTON & INDIANAPOLIS

© 1992 by Bill E. Lawson and Howard McGary

All rights reserved

No part of this book may be reproduced or utilized in any form or by
any means, electronic or mechanical, including photocopying and
recording, or by any information storage and retrieval system, without
permission in writing from the publisher. The Association of American
University Presses' Resolution on Permissions constitutes the only
exception to this prohibition.

The paper used in this publication meets the minimum requirements of American
National Standard for Information Sciences—Permanence of Paper for Printed
Library Materials, ANSI Z39.48-1984.

MANUFACTURED IN THE UNITED STATES OF AMERICA

Library of Congress Cataloging-in-Publication Data

McGary, Howard, date
    Between slavery and freedom : philosophy and American slavery / by
Howard McGary, Bill E. Lawson.
      p. cm.—(Blacks in the diaspora)
    Includes bibliographical references (p.   ) and index.
    ISBN 0-253-33272-9 (cloth). – 0-253-20745-2 (pbk.)
    1. Slaves' writings, American—History and criticism. 2. Slavery—
United States. I. Lawson, Bill E., date. II. Title.
III. Series.
E444.M44   1992
306.3'62'0973—dc20   92-7738

2 3 4 5   96 95

I would like to dedicate this book to the memory of my parents, Myrtis and Howard; my grandmother, Mencie Jedkins; my wife, LaVern; my children, Mya and Gaston; and my brother and sisters.

—*Howard McGary*

I would like to dedicate this book to my parents, Edmond and Annie Lawson; my wife, Barbara; my son, William; and my brothers and sisters.

—*Bill Lawson*

Article XIII

Sec. 1. Neither slavery nor involuntary servitude, except as a punishment for crime whereof the party shall have been duly convicted, shall exist within the United States or any place subject to their jurisdiction.

Sec. 2. Congress shall have power to enforce this article by appropriate legislation.

Article XIV

Sec. 1. All persons born or naturalized in the United States, and subject to the jurisdiction thereof, are citizens of the United States and of the State wherein they reside. No State shall make or enforce any law which shall abridge the privileges or immunities of citizens of the United States; nor shall any State deprive any person of life, liberty, or property, without due process of law; nor deny to any person within its jurisdiction the equal protection of the laws.

The United States Constitution

Contents

PREFACE

Between Slavery and Freedom is a work that has been percolating for many years. As a graduate student at the University of Minnesota in the early 1970s, I had the good fortune of discussing slavery and slave narratives with Ralph Crowder, then a talented graduate student in history. After reading numerous slave narratives, I was struck by what the slaves had to say about slavery and the slave experience. These narratives gave me new insights and caused me to rethink claims about slavery that I took to be obviously true.

I began to collect and read various sources on slavery and audited a graduate seminar on the topic. This research only increased my enthusiasm for knowledge on American chattel slavery. At the same time, I was working my way through a graduate program in philosophy at the University of Minnesota. In the early seventies these two activities seemed unrelated. Philosophy was one thing and research on slavery was another. When, however, I was asked to create and teach a course on philosophy and black experience in the department of philosophy at the University of Illinois, Chicago, in 1972, I began to explore the philosophical issues involved in the subject of slavery. It was at this point that the idea of philosophical examination of the issues raised by slavery merged with the exploration of the history of slavery.

As luck would have it, my colleague at the University of Illinois, Irving Thalberg, in addition to being a first-rate philosopher, was an avid reader of African-American history and culture. Conversations with Thalberg made it clear that there were issues connected with the American slavery experience that needed to be addressed philosophically.

I taught courses on philosophy and the black experience at both the University of Illinois and Rutgers University. In these courses, I examined such issues as slave resistance, paternalism and slavery, and personal identity. The need to write on philosophy and slavery using the slave narratives became even more important after reading Henry Louis Gates and Charles T. Davis's work on these sources (*The Slaves' Nar-*

rative, 1985). The idea gelled even more when I met my coauthor, Bill Lawson.

Howard McGary

I became interested in philosophy and the black experience while a graduate student at the University of North Carolina, Chapel Hill. I benefited from being able to discuss the writings of nineteenth-century black political theorists with a fellow graduate student, Wakesa Madzimoyo, a speech and communications major studying the speeches of antebellum black nationalist thinkers.

While my interest in slavery intensified, I continued to research the topic in a nonsystematic manner. In 1978, prior to completing my dissertation, I was asked to teach a course on Pan-Africanism. This course and my work with Paul Ziff, a noted philosopher of language, made me appreciate the power of language in our moral discourse. My philosophic research focused on understanding what is meant by certain political terms like political obligations and oppression. I wanted to understand these terms in the light of the insights gained from a reading of the history of black Americans.

At Spelman College, I was asked to teach on philosophy and the black experience. During this period, I invited members of diverse black nationalistic groups—The Republic of New Africa, The Original Hebrew Israelites, The Shrine of the Black Madonna, and others—to speak in my class. I was struck by the differing uses of the slavery experiences to explain and justify programs to alleviate the oppression of blacks in America. These various claims prompted me to study American slavery further. My research on slavery and political obligations continued when I accepted an appointment at Montclair State College.

In 1983 I met Howard and discovered that we both had a deep interest in slavery and how it affected the formulation of ethical and social concepts. Howard asked me if I would like to coauthor a book on slavery which addressed our mutual philosophical concerns. Thus the collaboration began.

The work started out as a philosophical examination of two slave narratives: *My Bondage and Freedom* by Frederick Douglass and *Twelve Years a Slave* by Solomon Northup. Along the way we realized that there were some recurring concepts that needed to be examined. The decision was made to examine several crucial ethical and social notions armed with what we took to be valuable but neglected insights gained from slave narratives as well as commentaries on slavery and philosophic analysis. This work is the result of our labor. We would like to thank Darleen Clark Hine for her support and encouragement.

Bill Lawson

Portions of chapter 3 were published as "The Concept of Resistance: Black Resistance during Slavery" in Creighton Peden and James Sterba, eds., *Freedom, Equality, and Social Change* (Lewiston, N.Y.: Edwin Mellen Press, 1989). Portions of chapter 4 originally appeared as "Locke and the Legal Obligations of Black Americans" in *Public Affairs Quarterly* 3:3 (1989), and parts of chapter 5 originally appeared as "Nobody Knows Our Plight: Moral Discourse, Slavery, and Social Progress" in *Social Theory and Practice* 18:2 (1992). Chapter 6 was first published as "Forgiveness" in *American Philosophical Quarterly* 26:4 (1989).

ACKNOWLEDGMENTS

Throughout the various stages of this book, I have benefited from the comments of numerous individuals and from the support of Rutgers University. The comments of my colleagues Mary Gibson, Douglas Husak, and Brian McLaughlin are greatly appreciated.

I also want to thank the participants at the first Irving Thalberg memorial lectures for their comments on a version of the chapter on forgiveness. Thanks are also owed to the participants at philosophy colloquia at the College of Charleston, Union College, and the University of Minnesota for their comments on a version of the chapter on paternalism. Finally, a note of thanks to the participants at the second international conference on social philosophy at Colorado College for their insightful remarks on a version of the chapter on resistance.

A special debt is owed to the following: John Dolan, for believing in me at a time when it mattered most; the late Irving Thalberg, Jr., for his support and understanding of the relevance of philosophy to cultural experiences; Al Prettyman and the members of the New York Society for the Study of Black Philosophy, for providing a forum for discussing philosophy and the black experience; Myles Brand for his support and encouragement; and Laurence Thomas, for his friendship, encouragement, and philosophical advice through the years.

Finally, my thanks to my wife, LaVern, whose comments often caused me to rethink my conclusions and who in many other ways made the writing of this book possible.

Of course, none of the persons that I have acknowledged should be taken to endorse what I have argued in this book.

Howard McGary

My research for this project was aided by support from the University of Delaware. The comments of my colleagues David Haslett, Roy Sorenson, and Doug Stalker were greatly appreciated. A special note of thanks to Frank Dilley and Sandra Harding, who provided constant support and advice. A University of Delaware Faculty Research Grant provided financial support and travel funds. Provost Leon Campbell also provided research funds.

I was also aided by discussions with Henry West and Tom Stewart during my visit to Macalester College. John Rubio, Sharon Baker, Rod Stewart, and Carol Rudisell provided helpful comments. Renata Johnson was my eyes in the library. My chapter on moral discourse received helpful criticism from presentations at the Schomburg Library, the University of Connecticut, and Washington and Jefferson College, and from the editors of *Social Theory and Practice*. The chapter on citizenship received helpful comments from presentations at West Virginia University and Austin College, and from the editors of *Public Affairs Quarterly*.

A special debt is owed to the following for their friendship, support, encouragement, and philosophical advice through the years: Paul Ziff, Ernst Manasse, and Laurence Thomas. I also want to thank Julie Rainbow for her kindness and support.

While I had an interest in the American slave experience, it was Howard McGary who had the idea for the book. Thanks Bro!

Finally, I want to thank my wife, Barbara, for her support and my son, William, who always had a hug ready.

As with all works of this type, any errors, omissions, or mistakes are mine and should not be attributed to those I have acknowledged or thanked.

Bill Lawson

PHILOSOPHY AND AMERICAN SLAVERY:

An Introduction

HOWARD MCGARY AND BILL LAWSON

Slaves in the United States certainly ranked among the most powerless and oppressed people in modern times. Contrary to popular opinion, slaves reflected deeply on every aspect of the miserable state they were forced to endure. In the writings of slaves and former slaves, we find discussion and speculation on such concepts as oppression, paternalism, resistance, political obligation, citizenship, and forgiveness.[1] In this work, we will examine these six concepts as they relate to and bear on American chattel slavery. Each of the topics to be considered better illuminates the world of slaves, the aftermath of slavery on the political process, and the way we understand key moral and political notions.

Our study is novel because we not only use the skills characteristic of analytical philosophy to study these notions, but we also make use of illuminations gained from other disciplines. In particular we draw on the work of historians of slavery, but more importantly we focus on the narratives of former slaves. This work is not an analysis of the slave narratives, but rather an explication of insights derived from these texts. This approach will enable us to gain an understanding of a group of people who were prevented from publicly participating in the discourse of their times about issues of far-reaching importance.

The inclusion of the voices of former slaves by historians has changed the character of the discourse about slavery. We think that attention to these voices can be useful in gaining philosophical insight. It would be an overstatement to say that moral and social philosophers have completely ignored the American slave experience; they often use the institution of slavery to illustrate a case of a clear-cut moral wrong or injustice. But their accounts have tended to view slavery from the point of view of those in power rather than from the point of view of the powerless.[2] We hope we can remedy this shortcoming by listening to the voices of former slaves. In doing so, we will not refashion all of the concepts examined, but rather we will show how the slavery experience and its aftermath can help us develop a better understanding of these concepts. To our knowledge, this has never been done in any on-going, systematic manner.

Some may object that philosophers need not consider any particular experience because philosophy is "impartial" and "universal." Given this conception of philosophy, it is understandable why philosophers have not even attempted to examine or consider the slave's point of view. We disagree with such a conception of philosophy.

We think that a philosopher might aspire to universalist criteria in some sense and still be committed to taking account of matters that are essentially perspectival, such as the American slave experience. Often the moral issues one focuses on depend on one's sensitivity to the actual experience of those involved. When one takes the slave experience seriously, issues like oppression and forgiveness come to the fore. But thinking seriously and reflectively about these issues, taking full account of the slave's experience, does not, so far as we can see, preclude aiming at universality or impartiality (or, for that matter, objectivity). It would be limiting if one were interested solely in how things seem from that perspective, but one can hardly appreciate the moral issues involved in American slavery without examining, *inter alia,* how things seemed from the slave's point of view.

This is not to say that the experiences of the oppressed and the downtrodden have not been the focus in some analyses. But even quite sympathetic accounts of the condition of slaves are still presented from the perspective of those with power and privilege. This perspective is not surprising, since the majority of works on the downtrodden or oppressed have not focused on the writings of those most intimately involved in the experiences.

So it is understandable that analytic moral and political philosophers have been concerned with concepts like liberty, distributive justice, punishment, power, and authority. If you have authority and power, then you need to know what it means to distribute goods and services justly, what constitutes just punishment, and what the proper relationship between state authority and the freedom of the individual is. On the other hand, terms like forgiveness, oppression, and resistance are far more likely to capture the attention of those who are powerless in society. If you are powerless, you need to understand oppression, why and how to resist it, and what the demands of forgiveness are. It is not surprising that examinations of these concepts have not been undertaken by those in the mainstream of contemporary analytical philosophy. These concepts, for the most part, have attracted the attention of religious thinkers and those who are thought to be on the fringes of philosophy. We hope to show that there is much to be learned by approaching the perspective of slaves with the skills characteristic of analytical philosophy to examine these concepts and notions.

The Significance of the Slave Narrative

It has been established by studies in a variety of academic disciplines that slave narratives have historical as well as literary and social value. Yet we still find that any attempt to write about a subject as controversial as slavery is sure to raise concerns about which sources give us the most accurate account of the slave experience. There has been and remains some debate on the reliability of sources. If, for example, we examine the writings of Ulrich B. Phillips on the antebellum slave system, we find a reliance on the plantation records kept by the slave owners.[3] The views of the slave owner and those of slaves on the nature of the slave system, however, were not often the same. Thus it was argued by Blassingame and others that in order to understand the nature of slavery and its effects on blacks it is necessary to examine the writings and tales of the slaves themselves.[4] Recent research in the area of slave narratives and letters has led to a better understanding of the life of the slave. By heeding the voices of slaves, we are able to get a feel for the time as well as a good sense of how the policies and practices affected those persons most intimately involved in slave society.

The writers used different styles of exposition to describe the slave experience.[5] Some narratives presented extremely eloquent accounts of slavery, while others have rendered very modest accounts both in terms of form and structure. Although some narratives are better than others, they all help to give us some insight into America's most brutal and peculiar institution.

The slave narrative, as a reflection of social history, has been praised as well as condemned.[6] Those who praise it argue that it helps to minimize problems of interpretation concerning such things as the nature of the slave community and the slaves' response to slavery.[7] Those who condemn slave narratives do so because the literature is so varied in terms of style, purpose, and competence of the author that it is not reliable as a source. Still others contend that since the most illuminating and penetrating narratives were written by authors who did not exemplify the typical slave, we should also question their reliability as a source of study. This approach, however, leads to another concern: the authenticity of the accounts of former slaves. What is to count as valid source material from the slave's point of view? This concern has led some writers, such as Blassingame, to examine the letters of former slaves along with the various narratives published before and after the Civil War.[8]

Not all narratives have been found to be authentic.[9] Some were written by free blacks who never experienced the pains of slavery.[10] Others were not written by blacks at all.[11] But these facts should not deter the diligent scholar from tilling the fertile field of slave literature. As with any other historical body of literature, scholars will have to weed out the good from the bad and the authentic from the non-authentic. Fortunately, a great deal of scholarship has already turned to this problem. Some critics, however, still maintain that even authentic and exceptional narratives should not be trusted. Gilbert Osofsky has responded most aptly to this criticism. He writes:

> Douglass presents a many-sided depiction of the slave experience—his is no papier-mâché book or antislavery tract. The historian who fails to use such a book or the narratives of a Bibb, a Brown, a Northup, or a Samuel Ringgold Ward because they are "exceptional" men might as well argue that Claude Brown and Eldridge Cleaver are unsuitable commentators on today's ghetto. To exclude the "exceptional" is to eliminate all strong autobiography as a distortion of the events of its time. Yet it is these writers whose books are most likely to interpret reality with insight and clarity.[12]

Not to avail ourselves of narratives by exceptional slaves would be a great mistake. Although certain slaves were more articulate and literate than others, it does not follow that their slave experiences were untypical.[13]

Finally, it should be noted that it is clear that some of the antebellum narratives were written to be used as moral persuaders against the evil of slavery. Does this knowledge negate their value as resource material for understanding the slave experience? We think that it does not.

Why Are the Narratives Philosophically Interesting?

The writings of former slaves not only provide an excellent account of the slave experience, they also show that the authors engaged in speculation about the moral implication of slavery. As philosophers, we will engage in philosophical analysis about their speculations.

It is not our contention that one will find a clear-cut and well-articulated discussion of these concepts in the various narratives that we draw on. The narratives, however, provide important insights that will enable us to rethink our views about certain concepts. An analysis of the problems and solutions as they are expressed from the mouths of slaves is interesting in its own right, but it is of particular interest, we will argue, because many of the concerns that are brought to the fore have created and shaped problems in contemporary society.

The Politics of Research on Slavery

Research on slavery in the United States has attracted scholars from a variety of disciplines. Needless to say, there have been heated debates within and across disciplines about the nature and effects of American slavery on those directly involved in the peculiar institution as well as those who live with its legacy.[14] For the most part, the debate over slavery has been led by historians, but one should not underestimate the role that scholars from other disciplines have played in shaping our understanding of the slave experience and how this scholarship has led to new moral and social insights.[15]

One historical work on American slavery and its effects that has triggered a plethora of articles and books from various disciplines is Stanley Elkins's *Slavery*. This work, published more than two decades ago, is a must for those who explore the topic. Unlike any other single work, Elkins's book bridged the gap between work done on slavery by historians, psychologists, and sociologists. Elkins's controversial conclusions and strategies of argument not only created intellectual interest in the topic but also raised significant political concerns. Perhaps the most provocative of Elkins's conclusions is his claim that the American "closed system" of slavery created among slaves what he labels the "Sambo" personality. By the "Sambo" personality Elkins means a slave who was docile but irresponsible, loyal but lazy, and characteristically child-like.[16] The idea of a unique personality type being created by slavery raised a number of questions. Many scholars questioned the existence of such a personality type, while others who did not question its existence argued about its cause(s).

No research is done in a political vacuum; Elkins's work and that of his critics is no exception. The idea of a "Sambo" personality caused scholars and laymen alike to question the consequences that such an observation, regardless of its truth or falsity, would have on blacks who still suffer from racial prejudice and discrimination. Some scholars have argued that the idea of "Sambo" only supported the negative stereotypical beliefs that many whites held about blacks.[17] Others have argued that the existence of such a personality is a myth that supports blaming the victims of slavery for their own victimization.[18] We believe that a clear understanding of the concepts of resistance and political obligation will require a careful examination of Elkins's "Sambo" thesis.

The Issues

The slave narrative as a literary and a philosophical source can be extremely rewarding. As we will show, this literature is not only moving as a historical account of the predicament of slaves but also as a vehicle for presenting and exploring several perplexing philosophical issues. What we will show is that the slave experience contributes some important insights to the quest for conceptual knowledge and understanding.

Our work will be guided by the recognition that research findings and even the examination of certain issues have far-reaching social and political ramifications. We begin with the belief that slavery was profoundly wrong morally, but we are open to an examination of the various arguments which seek to give us insight into the slave system and which may give us a better understanding of slavery and its effects.

In chapter 1, we discuss the question: what made slavery oppressive? It is clear that slaves saw the system of slavery as oppressive, and yet commentators on the slave experience have presented differing positions on the nature of the oppression. Some have defined oppression as the psychological indoctrination of the enslaved,[19] while others have focused on their alienation. Still others have counted the cruelty of the experience as the crux of the oppressiveness of slavery. In the narratives, slaves identify ownership as the mark of oppression. While the slaves saw the claim of ownership as the identifying mark of oppression, the moral implication of the claim of ownership is played down by many important commentators on slavery.[20] From our readings of the narratives, we will show that slavery was a social practice, and as such had rules and guidelines for the behavior of both blacks and whites. Crucial to an understanding of slavery is the role of the government in fostering and maintaining slavery as a social practice. Slaves were clearly victims of oppression and understood the nature of their oppression.[21]

The next topic that we shall consider is the problem of paternalism as manifested in the American slavery system. Paternalism has generally been defined as protecting the individual from self-inflicted harm or as promoting that individual's own good by overriding the individual's autonomy.[22] Some scholars have argued that slavery should be understood in terms of a paternalistic model.[23] We reject paternalistic explanations of slavery by showing that such accounts do not square with the facts and are confused as well.

One hotly contested claim arising out of the debates over the "Sambo" personality is the view that such a personality prevented resistance to slavery. Some scholars have even concluded that the "Sambo" personality helped to prolong slavery in this country. Others have strongly disagreed.[24] They deny the existence of "Sambo" as a general personality type and they reject the claim that slaves did not resist slavery. In chapter 3, we will challenge the claim that slaves' personalities were incapable of resistance.

In order to provide a thoughtful answer to the question, "Did slaves resist?," we need to: (1) have a clear idea of what we mean by "resistance"; and (2) have some criteria for determining whether certain actions of individuals and groups count as acts of resistance. In the case of slavery, we cannot simply ask the slaves themselves. So it would appear that we would have to depend upon such things as the slave narrative and the writings of persons who had first-hand information about the activities of slaves. But it may be presumptuous to think that the best evidence for the claim that slaves resisted would come from the slaves themselves or persons close to them. We will not be so presumptuous in our study. We will examine the writings of slaves critically, with an eye toward answering our question about resistance, but we will not assume that an answer could not come from other sources.

The "Sambo" concept or image also raises questions regarding the political obligations of the formerly enslaved person, particularly since the liberal democratic model presupposes that the individual who consents to the state has a certain moral status. If indeed blacks were "Sambos," then their status as free, consenting individuals would be called into question. While this issue has received scant attention in the philosophic literature, the philosopher Harvey Natanson has argued that, because of slavery and its aftermath, some blacks are not obligated to obey the laws of the state because they have not consented nor received the political protection that other fully free members of the state had.[25] Drawing his conclusion from his reading of Locke's political theory and his understanding of the slave experience, Natanson contends that some blacks are still in a state of nature and are not genuine citizens of the state. In chapter 4, we shall argue that this conclusion is false—that, given an accurate account of the slave experience, most blacks were in a position to give their consent, and furthermore that Natanson misreads Locke and thereby misconstrues the legal status of black Americans.

In the case of black Americans, the slavery experience must be taken into account in any discussion of state membership. Yet, the impact of slavery on the political and social status of blacks is often played down. We think that one reason this is so is that liberal democratic theory lacks a term for expressing the effects of enslavement. The absence of such a term means that little credence is given to arguments that draw on the slavery experience to provide support for either compensation or reparation for blacks. That is, there is no moral term for looking back to redress the past inequalities that affect the present social and political standing of blacks. In chapter 5, we argue that liberal democratic theory has a functional gap and an ensuing lexical gap because of a failure to appreciate the impact of slavery. Filling this gap would provide the moral grounding for correctly articulating the impact of the slavery experience on former slaves and their descendants, and it would also provide the framework for social programs that will move blacks beyond mere formal citizenship.

Given the brutality of slavery and the assault on the humanity of those held as slaves, it is remarkable that so many slaves were able to emerge from this brutal institution as moral agents. By moral agents, we mean persons who have a sense of right/wrong, good/bad, and who are able to evaluate from a moral point of view their own actions as well as the actions of others. What is just as remarkable is the fact that so many slaves were able to keep themselves psychologically intact. Some commentators have attempted to explain this fact by claiming that slavery was not as brutal as it has been made out to be, or by claiming that the black "Sambo" personality enabled slaves to endure things that would have broken persons with a secure sense of pride and self-worth. In the final chapter, we argue that the ability of slaves to forgive their oppressors played a crucial role in keeping slaves morally and psychologically whole. However, we argue that a very different and non-voluntaristic account of forgiveness best explains its nature and content in the lives of chattel slaves.

The voluntaristic model of forgiveness claims that when people have "good reasons" for forgiving, they will forgive.[26] We argue that forgiveness is closely tied to a person's feelings, and as such, the person is not always in a position to forgive even when there are good reasons for doing so. According to our account, forgiveness involves transforming not only the way we *think* about a person who has wronged us, but more importantly, the way we *feel* about a wrongdoer. We contend that forgiveness is a virtue, but that persons do not have a duty to forgive a wrongdoer when duty is correlated with a right to be forgiven. We argue that a person can forgive for "self-pertaining" reasons, where self-pertaining reasons are non-selfish, but self-regarding reasons that allow a person to remain psychologically whole.

Finally, we argue that the slave experience helps us to see how oppressed and powerless persons may be motivated to forgive for quite different reasons from the powerful. Oppressed people have to be especially concerned about whether their willingness to forgive signals a lack of self-respect.

Between Slavery and Freedom

One.
Oppression and Slavery

BILL LAWSON

I N 1850 Virginia planter George Fitzhugh wrote:

The slaves are all well fed, well clad, have plenty of fuel, and are happy.
They have no dread of the future—no fear of want. [The slaveholder] is
the least selfish of men.
   The institution of slavery gives full development and full play to the
affections.[1]

Fitzhugh was not alone in his opinions. There were many apologists
for chattel slavery in the United States.[2] Most historians of the American slave experience, however, have concluded that slaves were oppressed, although they disagree over what the mark of oppression was
during slavery. Some, like Stanley Elkins in his influential work *Slavery: A Problem in American Institutional and Intellectual life,* have defined
the mark of oppression as the psychological damage done to slaves.[3]
Others, such as Frank Tannenbaum and Orlando Patterson, have focused on slaves' alienation.[4] Kenneth Stampp saw the cruel treatment
of slaves as the defining mark of slavery.[5] Finally, commentators such
as James Oakes claim that the role of the government in keeping slaves
oppressed was the defining feature of slavery.[6]
   When, however, we examine what the slaves had to say about their
own oppression in slave narratives, ownership of human beings was
identified as the mark of oppression.[7] Unfortunately, most commentators have played down the moral implications of owning another human being. I think that slaves understood the institution of slavery and

correctly identified the concept of human ownership as the mark of their oppression. I shall make use of Frederick Douglass's paradoxical remark that ex-slaves were more oppressed after emancipation than during slavery in my argument that ownership was the defining feature of oppression for slaves.

Most philosophers and social scientists have attempted to define the term "oppression" with an eye to its etymological root: to press. When one is oppressed, one is "pressed down": one's position is made lower, or one is held in a lowly state.[8]

If we take this as our working definition of oppression, we can see why psychological indoctrination and alienation, cruelty, and unjust acts by the government can be oppressive. Still, I want to argue that they are not the defining marks of American chattel slavery. Psychological indoctrination and alienation, cruelty, and unjust acts by the government are important features of slavery, but none of these give American chattel slavery its distinctive twinge. Why is this so?

Psychological Indoctrination and Slavery

Possibly the best-known work with the premise that psychological indoctrination was the defining mark of slavery is Elkins's book. It was Elkins's contention that psychological indoctrination was a direct result of the closed nature of the slavery system: the restrictions on the behavior of slaves were so tightly enforced that the personality of blacks became deformed. Elkins used the "Sambo thesis" to explain the manner in which blacks had been psychologically indoctrinated by the slavery system:

Sambo, the typical plantation slave, was docile but irresponsible, loyal but lazy, humble but chronically given to lying and stealing; his behavior was full of infantile silliness and his talk with childish exaggerations. His relationship with his master was one of utter dependence and childlike attachment: it was indeed this childlike quality that was the very key to his being.[9]

Elkins argued that the behavior exhibited by slaves was similar to that of concentration camp prisoners. What is important for us here are Elkins's tests for a non-Sambo personality. Acts such as resistance, suicide, and hatred, according to Elkins, were exhibited by few slaves.

Thus, he concluded that they were "Sambos." Needless to say, Elkins's thesis has been the subject of much debate.

John Blassingame has argued that the "Sambo" personality was role-playing by slaves and that it should be viewed as one of three white stereotypes of slaves—the others being rebellious Nat and tricky Jack.[10] Blassingame contended that the system was not as closed as Elkins contends. Slaves, he argues, developed their own culture within the slave society.[11] This culture was dedicated to achieving freedom. As Stampp wrote: "Slaves showed great eagerness to get some—if they could not get all—of the advantages of freedom."[12] Accommodating behavior by slaves had to be understood in the context of the lives they were forced to live: "If slaves yielded to authority most of the time, they did so because they usually saw no other practical choice."[13] Slaveholders understood this and worked to construct a system that would make slaves stand in fear.

If Blassingame and other historians are correct, their conclusions call into question Elkins's thesis of a "Sambo" personality. If by psychological indoctrination we mean that slaves were made into "Sambos," and if there were non-Sambos as Elkins claims, then psychological indoctrination cannot have been the defining feature of slavery. It is not surprising, however, that Elkins fails to see that slaves did pass his test for being non-Sambos. In chapters 3 and 6, we will see why some commentators fail to appreciate the various forms of resistance by slaves and why the surprising lack of hatred and resentment in the slave narratives should not be interpreted as meekness or compliance.

One can hold that psychological indoctrination is the defining mark of slavery without endorsing the "Sambo" thesis. Some might argue that psychological indoctrination could have occurred during slavery without producing "Sambos." If this is true, psychological indoctrination could still be the defining mark of American chattel slavery. People who take this position most often claim that psychological indoctrination leads to alienation and that this alienation was the mark of oppression during slavery.

Alienation and Slavery

Sociologist Orlando Patterson thinks that alienation was the defining mark of slavery. Like Elkins, Patterson claims that the system of slavery was closed, but, unlike Elkins, he does not believe that the closed system created a "Sambo" personality. Patterson believes that slaves suffered from "natal alienation," defined as:

the loss of ties of birth in both ascending and descending generations. It also has the important nuance of loss of native status, of deracination. It was this alienation of the slave from all formal, legally enforceable ties of "blood," and from any attachment to groups or localities other than chosen for him by the master, that gave the relation of slavery its peculiar value to the master.[14]

Patterson develops this view of the slave from a comparative study of slavery in the United States and other parts of the world. He was looking for the essential features of any slave system. Perhaps his failure to appreciate alternative accounts of the psychological condition of the slave can be attributed to his global perspective.[15] Reading American slave narratives, one quickly observes that many of the features of Patterson's "natal alienation" thesis are not found.[16] Again, if one looks at the work of Blassingame, Stampp, and Stuckey[17] on the slave community, one questions whether slaves in the United States suffered from "natal alienation." Any attempt to use alienation as a defining feature of American chattel slaves must discount the contrary evidence found in slave narratives. What we do find in the commentaries on slavery and in slave narratives is the various forms of cruel treatment that slaves were forced to endure. This has led some people to conclude that cruelty was the defining mark of slavery.

Cruelty and Slavery

When we examine the slave narratives, it is clear that cruelty was an important feature of slavery. Slave narratives are replete with examples of the cruelty of slaveholders. Slaves were brutalized physically and subjected to psychological abuse. Slaves were subject to the whims of their master or mistress. This cruel treatment of slaves did cause their position to be lower than that of the slaveholders and nonslaves. Yet there was a wide range of behaviors exhibited by slaveholders toward their slaves. This behavior ranged from unbelievable cruelty to clearly humanitarian treatment. But even though slaveholders could be kind, slaves knew that cruelty was a mechanism available to the slaveholder for keeping them in check.

Frederick Douglass's story of his being sent to Covey, the negro-breaker, is an excellent example of the use of the threat of cruelty and then actual cruel treatment to keep slaves under control.[18] Female slaves were not spared the cruelty of slavery. The cruel treatment of Linda Brent is well known.[19] The knowledge that cruel behavior could be exhibited by the slaveholder to keep control may be thought to show that cruelty was the defining feature of slavery.

Historian Kenneth Stampp thought that it was. He saw cruelty as a way to break the will of the slave. The cruel treatment of slaves reinforced the idea that slaves had no control over the most intimate aspects of their lives. Slaves could be forced to have sexual intercourse and then endure the pain of being separated from their children with little regard for the psychological or physical welfare of either. As a consequence of the cruel behavior of slaveholders, a social etiquette of race relations developed which had as its sole purpose the social control of slaves.[20] All of these actions were designed to make the slave "stand in fear" and to reinforce the position that slaves were chattel.

But it is clear that some slaves were never treated cruelly. Some slaveholders were troubled by the institution of slavery. Patrick Henry wrote: "Every thinking honest man rejects slavery in speculation, how few in practice? Would anyone believe that I am Master of slaves of my own purchase? I am drawn along by the general inconvenience of living without them; I will not, I cannot justify it."[21] Henry's remark should not be taken to imply that like-minded slaveholders sold or freed their slaves. But as remarks by Douglass and other ex-slaves show, there were some humane (if that is the correct word) slaveholders. This would not defeat, however, the claim that the defining feature of slavery was its cruelty. Remarks like those of Douglass only show that not all slaveholders were cruel.

If Stampp's position can be interpreted to mean that slavery was the cruelest of cruel institutions, then this would be a consistent position. But Stampp also claims that at the end of slavery "all blacks lost were their chains."[22] By this Stampp seems to mean that blacks were treated just as cruelly after emancipation. We find similar claims in the writings of Frederick Douglass. If Douglass and Stampp are right about the cruel treatment of blacks after slavery, and if cruelty is the defining mark of slavery, then either slavery continued after emancipation or cruelty is not its defining mark.

Of course, one may want to claim that given the continuation of cruel treatment, blacks were still enslaved. This position is consistent but counter-intuitive. After my discussion of human ownership as the defining feature of slavery, I will show why cruelty cannot be the defining feature. But for now let us turn to the claim that the mark of slavery was the government's role in establishing and maintaining the subjugation of blacks.

Governmental Action and Slavery

Historian James Oakes argues that American chattel slavery was dependent upon the political system, not the reverse. Oakes admits that the relationship between slaveholders and the legal system was paradoxical: "the fact that slaves were 'totally' subordinate to the masters did not mean that the master's power over the slave was absolute."[23] The state regulated the behavior of slaveholders toward their slaves. Citing John Codman Hurd, Oakes gives the following definition of slavery: "that condition of a natural person, in which, by the operation of law, the application of his physical and mental powers depends, as far as possible, upon the will of another who is himself subject to the supreme power of the state."[24] How much power did the state have? Oakes thinks that beyond bringing slavery into existence, "the government's role in regulating and maintaining the master-slave relationship was essential."[25] The state provided guidelines for who could and could not be a slave.

Consider the situation of black women during slavery. At one point in American history, both blacks and whites could be held in bondage. Then, as early as 1604, some owners adopted the practice of considering blacks, and the children of bound black women slaves for life, even before it was part of the legal system. This put the relative advantages of white and black bondage in a different light.[26]

Of all the discriminatory practices of slavery, the concept of *partus sequitur ventrem*—that the child follows the condition of the mother—was the most damaging. It put the stamp of social inferiority on children born to black women regardless of the race of the father and put a premium on childbearing. This practice also kept the institution of slavery alive.

By the time Linda Brent published her narrative, the concept of *partus sequitur ventrem* was established law. Brent wrote:

Sometime, when my master found that I refused to accept what he called his kind offers, he would threaten to sell my child. "Perhaps that will humble you," said he.

Humble me! Was I not already in the dust? But his threat lacerated my heart. I knew the law gave him power to fulfil it; for slaveholders have been cunning enough to enact that "the child shall follow the condition of the mother," not the father; thus taking care that licentiousness shall not interfere with avarice. . . . When they told me my new-born babe was a girl, my heart was heavier than it had ever been before. Slavery is terrible for men; but it is far more terrible for women.[27]

The power of the state, according to Oakes, was overwhelming and the slaveholders "never seriously questioned the state's right to say who was a slave." One reason the state's codification of black slavery was accepted was that it was just assumed that "slaves should be Negroes and Negroes should be slaves." Oakes notes: "This was the universal supposition by the eighteenth century, and it served to mask the awesome implications of authority the state exercised when it codified that presumption."[28]

The state also had the job of defining who was a "Negro." Miscegenation raised a problem for those persons who believed in racial purity. Where genetics failed,

the law stepped in to provide official sanction as well as clarification for a powerful cultural proposition. . . . "Every person who has one-fourth, or other larger part, of negro blood, shall be deemed a mulatto," the Kentucky legislature decreed in 1852, "and the word negro, when used in any statute, shall be construed to mean mulatto as well as negro."[29]

The government also regulated the conditions under which slaves could be set free. In addition, the government could confiscate slaves for non-payment of taxes and take slaves if the slaveholder was convicted of a criminal offense. And finally, the state could set limits on what the masters could do to slaves, but such laws often permitted far from humane treatment.[30] For example, Moses Roper wrote in his narrative:

This is according to law: after three call they may shoot a runaway slave. Soon after the one on horse came up with me, catching hold of the bridle of my horse, pushed a pistol to my side; the others soon came up, and breaking off several of the branches from the trees, they gave me one hundred blows. This they did near the planter's house. The gentleman was not at home, but his wife came out and begged them not to *kill me so near the house*.[31]

According to Oakes, slavery could not survive without some legal recognition of its existence: some legal determination of who was and who was not a slave and some rudimentary definition of slavery itself.[32]

When we examine the role of the government, we find a better candidate for the mark of oppression during slavery. The effects of government sanctions, restrictions, and codes were everywhere. Individuals acted in ways that were cruel, harmful, and unjust, but the government played a crucial role in defining, enforcing, and maintaining the ways blacks were subjugated. Many scholars have called attention to this fact and have detailed the specific ways that the government sanctioned slavery. What is often missing from their account, however, is the importance that slaves attached to the government-supported view that blacks were chattel.

This is not to say that commentators have not recognized that holding slaves as property had serious consequences, but rather that they failed to see that government support for the idea of blacks as property distinguished American chattel slavery from other oppressive systems. What makes slavery in the United States distinctive is the fact that slaves were viewed solely as property. As such, they had no private existence. This important fact did not go unnoticed by the slaves. You find them again and again calling attention to the distinctiveness of a system that perceives human beings as objects, as property to be bought, sold, or exchanged like any other commodity.

Examples of slaves' consciousness of their status as property can be found in slave narratives. In the 1930s some of the remaining former slaves were interviewed about the slavery experience. James Martin recalls: "The slaves were put into stalls like pens they used for cattle—a man and his wife with a child on each arm. And there's a curtain, sometimes just a sheet over the front of the stall, so the bidders can't see the 'stock' too soon."[33] Nearly one hundred years earlier, Lunsford Lane wrote emotionally about his coming to realize his slave status in his youth: "To know, also, that I was never to consult my own will, but was entirely under the control of another, was a state of mind hard for me to bear. Indeed all things now made me *feel*, what I had only known in words, that *I was a slave*."[34] Linda Brent wrote in 1861 about the attitudes of many southern women regarding slaves: "Southern woman often marry a man knowing that he is the father of many little slaves. They do not trouble themselves about it. They regard such children as property, as marketable as the pigs on the plantation."[35]

In the 1849 narrative of James W. C. Pennington, we find a clear statement of the slaves' understanding of the oppressiveness of slavery:

You cannot constitute slavery without the chattel principle—and with the chattel principle you can not save it from these results. Talk not then about kind and Christian masters. They are not masters of the system. The system is master of them; and the slaves are their vassals.[36]

Slaves were well aware of what made their condition oppressive. It might be claimed that the notion that ownership was the mark of oppression was just another way to say slavery was cruel. This would be a mistake. Slaves still viewed their condition as oppressive even when the slaveholders were kind. Slaves understood that regardless of the treatment they received from slaveholders, human ownership was the crux. We have focused on the views of slaves, but another way to highlight the importance of the concept of ownership in the slavery experience is to contrast the condition of slaves with that of freed blacks during slavery.

Freedmen and Oppression

In the antebellum United States, oppression was not limited to slaves. Quite plainly the free black could not escape contamination from the concept of racial inferiority. When the black race came to be identified with slavery, the fortunes of the free blacks became indissolubly linked with the fortunes of the slaves. When blacks came to be regarded as subhuman, the concept applied with equal force to the blacks who were characterized as free.[37]

The term "freedman" did not accurately depict the social consequences of living in a racially stratified society. It was a term used to indicate those blacks who were not slaves. In reality, those blacks who were said to be freedmen had few rights that whites were bound to respect.

Those blacks who were manumitted during the antebellum period were faced immediately with the problem of trying to navigate a system of laws and customs that was designed to keep all blacks oppressed.[38] An example of the value placed on liberty for free blacks was stated in a Georgia law that declared:

The free person of color is entitled to no right of citizenship, except such as are specially given by law. His status differs from that of the slave in this: No master having dominion over him, he is entitled to the free use of his liberty, labor and property, except so far as he is restrained by law.

All laws enacted in reference to slaves, and in their nature applicable to free persons of color, shall be construed to include them, unless specially excepted.[39]

The intent of the government in the antebellum United States was to maintain a social, political, and economic gap between blacks and whites. The condition of subjugation was designed to exist as a permanent state for all blacks, regardless of their legal status.

What becomes clear from a reading of the literature about free blacks is that the color of a person's skin was the determining factor in his or her ability to provide a secure life outside the bonds of slavery. There was no connection between being a free black and social acceptance. The value of being considered a freedman was questioned as early as 1837 by the black editor Samuel Cornish. He wrote:

What an empty name. What a mockery. Free men indeed. When so unrighteously deprived of every civil and political privilege. Free indeed. When almost every honorable incentive to pursuit of happiness, so largely and so freely held out to his fairer brother, is withheld from him. A free man, when prejudice binds the most galling chains around him. Drives him from every mechanical employment, and situations of trust, or emolument, frowns him from doors of our institutions of learning; forbids him to enter every public place of amusement, and follows him wherever he goes, pointing at him the finger of scorn and contempt. Is this to be a free man?[40]

In 1832, black political activist Maria Stewart declared:

I have asked several individuals of my sex, who transact business for themselves, if providing our girls were to give them the most satisfactory references, they would not be willing to grant them equal opportunity with others? Their reply has been—for their own part they had no objection; but as it was not the custom, were they to take them into their employ, they would be in danger of losing the public patronage.[41]

Cornish and Stewart realized that slaves and blacks designated as freedmen were oppressed. Most free blacks were subject to legal restrictions on their behavior which prevented them from closing the social, economic, and political gap existing between blacks and whites in the antebellum United States.

It was the rare exception when a black could improve his social and economic position in antebellum America. The fact that a few blacks were able to flourish during slavery and even own slaves[42] does not show that for the most part free blacks were not oppressed. John Hope Franklin, the noted historian, concludes that: "In the South free Negroes were nothing less than pariahs, while in the North they were an oppressed and underprivileged minority."[43]

Although free blacks were not property, they were subject to many of the same restrictions placed on slaves. As the narrative by Solomon Northup illustrates, free blacks always had to be on guard against being kidnapped into slavery. But not being chattel was still important because, if they were kidnapped and sold into slavery, their free status could be used to secure their release.[44]

One might think that many of the laws that governed the behavior of blacks in slavery were also applied to blacks out of slavery. This is a mistake. In the United States being enslaved meant that you were the legal property of another human being. This meant that those persons held as slaves were denied the right to consider themselves autonomous moral beings. The slaveholders felt justified in setting personal goals and directing the course of the lives of slaves. Slaves were denied any viable personal life. The most intimate aspects of their existence were decided upon by the slaveholder. They could be sold or given away at whim. While the state may have put some restrictions on the treatment of slaves, slaveholders still had a great deal of latitude in deciding how to treat their human property. If this analysis is correct, it is unclear how we should interpret Frederick Douglass's paradoxical remark that blacks after emancipation were in a worse condition than slaves.

Oppression after Slavery

Douglass had hoped that America would approach the tenets of the Declaration of Independence and the Constitution in its treatment of blacks after emancipation. Waldo Martin, in his work *The Mind of Frederick Douglass,* writes that Douglass thought that the peonage system blacks found themselves enmeshed in after emancipation made freedom a sham.[45] Douglass wrote:

That he is worse off, in many respects, than when he was a slave, I am compelled to admit, but I contend that the fault is not his, but that of his heartless accusers. He is the victim of a cunningly devised swindle, one which paralyzes his energies, suppresses his ambition, and blasts all his hopes; and though he is nominally free he is actually a slave. I here and now denounce his so-called emancipation as a stupendous fraud—a fraud upon him, a fraud upon the world.[46]

Douglass was so disgusted by the plight of blacks after emancipation, that while he was not an advocate of emigration schemes, he had to admit that, for some blacks, emigration might be the best alternative to life in America.

I had hope that the relations subsisting between the former slaves and the old master class would gradually improve; but while I believe this, and still have some such weak faith, I have seen enough, heard enough and learned enough of the condition of these people in South Carolina and Georgia to make me welcome any movement which will take them out of the wretched condition which I now know them to be. While I shall continue to labor for increased justice to those who stay in the South, I give you my hearty 'Godspeed' your emigration scheme. I believe you are doing a good work.[47]

Douglass had hope that emancipation would bring blacks and whites together in a new spirit of freedom and political equality. What he found instead was that blacks were denied civil rights and were physically unprotected. Douglass was disheartened because he thought it was shameful for the government to fail to protect citizens when it could.[48]

According to Douglass, emancipation had made the condition of blacks worse than that of slaves, because at least in slavery the slaveholder had a vested interested in looking out for the welfare of blacks. Stampp echoed Douglass's remark when he concluded that at emancipation "all blacks lost were their chains."[49]

It is understandable why some persons would believe that all blacks lost at the end of slavery were their chains. Many view the current oppression of blacks as slavery because a number of the same conditions that were the essential features of chattel slavery seem to be in place now. Sociologist Joe Feagin, for example, in his 1986 article "Slavery Unwilling to Die: The Background of Black Oppression in the 1980s," examines the life of slaves and concludes that present-day blacks are in a state of semi-slavery. Feagin argues that while there have been some political and social changes, for the most part the condition of blacks has not changed drastically since the 1600s.[50] I think that he is wrong. But, in order to understand why, we must come to some understanding of the political and social standing of blacks before and after emancipation.

Clearly, if we take Douglass's remark that emancipation was a sham to mean that blacks were still oppressed, then he was right. But if Douglass meant emancipation had no positive impact on the status of slaves, then he was wrong. The same can be said of Stampp's remark. A careful reading of slave narratives shows that slaves thought that emancipation was a crucial step in the process toward freedom. Strange as it may seem to some, blacks were in a better condition than they had been as slaves; blacks could no longer be owned.

The history of blacks after emancipation shows very clearly the failure of the United States government to protect blacks. Blacks were still oppressed. Yet, at the same time, they were legally citizens in what professed to be a liberal democratic state. Unfortunately many of the same sources of stratification that held when blacks were held as slaves continued after emancipation. When the shift from the oppressiveness of slavery to the oppression faced by blacks after emancipation is viewed in this manner, we can understand the tendency to want to call the situation of blacks after emancipation slavery. State actions in both forms of oppression are similar. This equation is wrong, however. Slavery was the oppression of individuals who were not United States citizens. Slavery in the United States was a situation in which blacks were viewed as property. The situation that blacks encountered after emancipation was the usurpation of the legitimate political power of one group of citizens by another.

Unfortunately, the failure of Reconstruction could very well lead one to underestimate the value of the Emancipation Proclamation. It is to be hoped that my discussion helps us to understand why persons who believed that slavery continued after emancipation are wrong.

As historian James Oakes notes, antebellum historian U. B. Phillips had remarked that the late nineteenth-century South was the same as the antebellum South. Oakes counters: "The prewar planters whose papers Phillips so diligently uncovered were not the landlord-merchants he had observed in his youth. The power and wealth of the antebellum masters had rested on their ownership of slaves."[51]

While blacks had to endure many of the same unjust acts after emancipation, they understood the value of not being owned as property. In chapter 4 it will be shown that some commentators on the slave experience think that the fact the United States government conferred citizenship on blacks denied blacks the right to choose citizenship, and that the denial of choice means blacks are not citizens.

Because many of the conditions of oppression that slaves faced and freedmen encountered were the same as those they faced after emancipation, we can understand what Stampp meant when he claimed all slaves lost were their chains and why Douglass thought emancipation a fraud. We also can understand why Feagin would think that blacks are in a condition of semi-slavery. Finally, however, we must conclude that, although the end of slavery did not spell the end of oppression, it was still a very important event. It had the effect of conferring on blacks a legitimate claim against the state. The Emancipation Proclamation and the Thirteenth, Fourteenth, and Fifteenth Amendments to the Constitution gave blacks the legal ammunition to fight Jim Crow laws and to push for full citizenship.[52] As historian Armstead L. Robinson notes: "These amendments eliminated chattel slavery as a racially exclusive legal category at the same time they conferred citizenship and voting rights upon Afro-American whether 'born' or 'shot' free."[53]

The political reality is that blacks were oppressed after emancipation but this oppression was the oppression of citizens. This oppression did have its roots in the slavery experience. In chattel slavery, however, whites could claim legal ownership of blacks.

Often emancipation is seen only for its political and social effect. But it should be remembered that emancipation also had a moral effect. It made null and void, morally and legally, the idea of owning another human in the United States. The legal right to own another human being was the essential feature in American chattel slavery. We must remember this fact when distinguishing American chattel slavery from other forms of oppression.

Two.
Paternalism and Slavery

HOWARD McGARY

How SHOULD we view those who were the principal actors during slavery? Were slaves "Sambos" who acquiesced in their own oppression, or were they psychologically whole persons who struggled to end their enslavement? On the other side of the equation, were slaveholders heartless, money-grubbing, evil persons who took delight in the enslavement of Africans, or were they merely pawns caught up in an evil system? These are complex questions. Slavery was a multi-faceted system. Thus, it is difficult to give a single description of slavery in the United States that captures all of its nuances. There has, however, been an intense debate over how the typical slave and slaveholder should be characterized.

One group of scholars has been reluctant to describe the typical slaveholder as evil.[1] These commentators argue that slaveholders had the best interest of slaves at heart. They describe slaveholders as misguided, ignorant, or morally weak. In other words, typical slaveholders held a set of false beliefs which caused them to act in what we now can see were morally objectionable ways. Others have argued that slaveholders appreciated that what they were doing was wrong, but they did it anyway in order to gain economic power and social privilege.[2]

This is a complex debate, and I shall not attempt to cover every facet of it. Instead, I shall focus on one aspect of this debate: whether or not slavery should be characterized as paternalistic. By a paternalistic explanation of slavery, I mean one that claims that slaveholders held slaves because they believed it was in the slaves' best interests, or an explanation that claims that slaves viewed their masters in a manner similar to the way children see their guardians. So described, the typical slaveholder was ignorant but not evil. A case often said to be analogous is the exploitation of women by men. In such cases, the behavior of males is objectionable, but the typical male is not thought to be evil. This is not to say that certain males, like certain slaveholders, were not evil, but only that evil does not describe the typical male or slaveholder.

In my view, paternalistic accounts of slavery cannot withstand close scrutiny. This became apparent to me from my reading of slave narratives, because slaves typically described slavery and their slaveholders in ways that called paternalism into question. In James Pennington's narrative *The Fugitive Blacksmith,* he writes:

My feelings are always outraged when I hear them speak of "kind masters"—"Christian masters,"—"the mildest form of slavery,"—"well fed and clothed slaves," as extenuations of slavery; I am satisfied they either mean to pervert the truth, or they do not know what they say. The being of slavery, its soul and body, lives and moves in the chattel principle, the property principle, the bill of sale principle; the cart-whip, starvation, and nakedness, are its consequences to a greater or less extent, warring with the dispositions of men.[3]

Some might say that the description of slavery as a paternalistic institution is clearly false, an attempt to put what is clearly objectionable in a better light. They are correct, but for reasons much more involved than one might imagine. Paternalistic accounts of slavery support the view that slavery was unjust, but that it was not as bad as some people have thought.

It would be foolish to contend that there were no positive human interactions between slaves and slaveholders, or that slaveholders had no motive for doing things that benefited slaves. Clearly, after the abolition of the slave trade in 1808, slaveholders had good self-interested reasons for looking out for the welfare of their slaves. Peter Parish, in *Slavery: History and Historians,* notes that a number of historians who defend paternalistic accounts of slavery make use of this fact.[4]

There is, however, a vast difference between providing slaves with the bare necessities to keep them productive and a sincere concern for their welfare. It is doubtful that providing a person with the bare necessities in order to keep them productive counts as paternalism. The motive for the slaveholder's behavior was his own good, not the good of his slaves. In fact, the slaveholders created the situation which made their alleged paternalism necessary. If I force persons into a situation where I have to meet their needs because it promotes my good, then I am not acting in a paternalistic manner.

I would like to make the strategy of this chapter clear. First, I offer reasons why scholars have offered paternalistic explanations of slavery. Next, I contend that all paternalistic justifications are captured by one of five basic models that I describe below. I then argue that none of these models describes the true relationship between slaves and slaveholders. Finally, I argue that paternalistic explanations of slavery are incompatible with our conceptions of what counts as evil. I would also like to make it clear that my aim is not to provide a new justification of paternalism, but to show that, given our present understanding of paternalism, all such defenses of American slavery fail.

Scholars on both sides of the paternalism debate claim that they are only describing or explaining the institution of American slavery, not excusing or justifying it. But, as we know, excuses and justifications are types of explanation, and we evaluate excuses and justifications much the same way as other explanations. Explanations in general answer questions about how or why something happened. Justifications are explanations that put behaviors in the best possible light.

How does the distinction between explanations, excuses, and justifications relate to historical accounts of slavery? I think that, given the intimate connection between explanations, excuses, and justifications, historical explanations can and sometimes do excuse or justify. With excuses, the person thought to be liable is willing to settle for an explanation that puts his behavior in a more favorable light. Imagine the following conversation between A and B:

A: Why did slaveholders hold slaves?
B: They did so in order to promote the slave's own good.

B's explanation also counts as an excuse and possibly as a justification for slaveholders' owning of slaves.

Even some scholars who include slave narratives among their sources have claimed that the relationship between the slaveholder and the slave was "paternalistic." For example, the noted historian of slavery Eugene Genovese writes:

For the slaveholders paternalism represented an attempt to overcome the fundamental contradiction in slavery: the impossibility of the slaves' ever becoming the things they were supposed to be. Paternalism defined the involuntary labor of the slaves as legitimate return to their masters for protection and direction. But the masters' need to see their slaves as acquiescent human beings constituted a moral victory for the slaves themselves. Paternalism's insistence upon mutual obligations—duties, responsibilities, and ultimately even rights—implicitly recognized the slave's humanity.[5]

Genovese goes on to say: "whenever paternalism exists, it undermines solidarity among the oppressed by linking them to the oppressors."[6]

Although Genovese clearly condemns the actions of the slaveholders, he still characterizes slavery in paternalistic terms. As the quotation above demonstrates, Genovese sees the paternalism of slavery as a viable explanation for the lack of solidarity among slaves. It is clear to me that Genovese does not intentionally wish to cast the slaveholders and the institution of slavery in a positive light, but some historians have deliberately used the paternalistic explanation to excuse slaveholders and slavery. For example, William K. Scarborough, in his article "Slavery—The White Man's Burden," writes:

Professor Genovese has elucidated with remarkable perception the paternalistic relationship which bound together masters and slaves in the Old South. My principal quarrel with his interpretation lies in his characterization of the planters, especially in his distressing propensity to assign to them only base and ignoble motives for acts of genuine benevolence.[7]

Genovese rejects Scarborough's position, but in the appendix to his book *Roll, Jordan, Roll* he makes it clear that he does see slavery as a paternalistic institution. He is quick to warn us, however, that "[t]he subordination of one race to another or the people of any country to a welfare state does not constitute a paternalistic order in any historically meaningful sense."[8]

Unfortunately, Genovese never gives us a clear statement of what he means by "paternalism." He does tell us what it is not; for example, the idea that the strong must protect and lead the weak in return for obedience and labor is not paternalistic. But one thing is clear from Genovese's perspective: paternalism requires coercion. He claims that paternalism is incompatible with bourgeois social relations. By this I take him to mean that the idea of individual autonomy is inconsistent with paternalism.

Genovese fails to see that paternalism in fact is not always incompatible with bourgeois social relations. As I shall argue in the final section of this chapter, paternalism has been and continues to be an acceptable and even heralded practice in liberal and bourgeois societies. Given the way that paternalism has been viewed in these societies, such explanations can serve to put what would normally be thought of as reprehensible behavior in a more positive light.

Why Paternalism?

Commentators who have adopted paternalistic accounts of the institution of slavery do so for several reasons. Generally, they believe that such accounts have a great deal of explanatory power. More specifically, they think these explanations allow us to understand and even to justify certain aspects of slave society not justifiable with nonpaternalistic explanations—for example, the apparent devotion that some slaves were said to show toward their masters. Viewing the slaveholder/slave relationship as paternalistic also gives the slave the status of human being, something denied by many whites during slavery. But even if it does, it came at great cost. In order for the slave to enjoy the alleged benefits of a paternalistic master, he had to give up all claims to respect as a responsible adult. He had to be a "Sambo."[9]

We should be careful to note that to say that slavery was paternalistic could mean several things. One could mean that all or most slaveholders thought that slavery was a good thing for the slaves. In other words, their motives for owning slaves was to promote and protect the slave's best interest. On the other hand, one could interpret paternalism in such a way that the motives of slaveholders were not the key issue, but rather that slavery was a state of dependency: that the slaves were dependent upon slaveholders for their survival and not capable of being responsible for their own fates. According to the 1850 argument of slavery apologist Dr. Samuel Cartwright of the University of Louisiana, slavery was necessary for the survival of Africans: "The African will starve rather than engage in a regular system of agricultural labor, unless impelled by the stronger will of the white man."[10]

This interpretation would obviously place slavery and the slaveholders in a more positive light. If we accept Cartwright's reasons for holding slaves, then we should view the behavior of slaveholders in less harsh terms and perhaps even excuse it. But clearly one primary reason why slaveholders held slaves was they believed that it was in their best interest to do so.[11] They often gave rationalizations which included concern for the welfare of the slave, but in the overwhelming majority of cases these explanations were just rationalizations for an oppressive system that worked to the advantage of the slaveholders.

But suppose we say that most slaveholders held slaves because they felt that they had no viable alternatives. In other words, slaveholders felt that they had to hold slaves because if they didn't, some harsher masters would.[12] They could thus contend that they were holding slaves for the slaves' own good. This argument fails for several reasons. First, it assumes that the profit motive did not play a crucial role in the slaveholder's decision to hold slaves. Second, it assumes that slavery was not a highly coordinated and collective activity.[13] Finally, it assumes that slaveholders felt that slavery was wrong, but nonetheless a kind of necessary evil. I think on any careful reading of the sources all three of these assumptions are false. Therefore any argument that has these assumptions as premises cannot be sound.

Critics might contend that (a) even if during slavery the facts did not support the slaveholder's paternalistic rationalizations of slavery, it does not follow that (b) slavery could not justifiably be given a paternalistic interpretation. If we think that paternalism is a function of an individual's operative beliefs, then (b) does not follow from (a). Suppose many slaveholders just didn't see the facts, even quite obvious ones? Let us say they were in some state that falls on the self-deception continuum. If the slaveholders were self-deceived about the extent to which slaves were capable of living autonomous lives, then (b) is false.

However, it is doubtful that many or most slaveholders held the false belief that slavery was a beneficent institution. Even though some apologists claimed that slavery was good for slaves, there is little, if any, evidence to support the strong claim that most or many slaveholders genuinely believed that they were helping blacks by holding them as slaves. No doubt there were some slaveholders who genuinely held such beliefs, but given the lack of evidence for this even in the eighteenth and nineteenth centuries, persons had to engage in severe self-deception in order to convince themselves that their motive for owning slaves was paternalistic.

My reading of the sources, particularly biographies, diaries, and letters of slaveholders, suggests that many of them self-consciously used the paternalistic view of slavery as mere rationalizations when confronted by the critics of slavery.[14] Perhaps the ones who did not were in a state of self-deception fueled by "motivated belief." One is in a state of motivated belief in believing that P if (1) one believes that P; and (2) the belief that P is causally sustained by a motive for believing that P. By "motive" I mean a mental state consisting of certain sorts of beliefs and desires. These beliefs and desires provide the subject with a rationale for doing something—in the case in question for believing that P.

Perhaps I can illustrate what I have in mind here by drawing upon what it means to have a favorable disposition toward someone you like a great deal. Having a positive disposition toward a person, in spite of evidence that would tend to support a negative attitude toward the person, involves what I call being in a state of motivated belief. This state can range from wishful thinking to full-blown self-deception. Being in a state of motivated belief directs one's attention away from negative evidence and causes one to exaggerate every small bit of evidence that speaks in the person's favor. When one has a negative disposition, just the opposite is true. For example, it may reveal itself phenomologically in the agent being irritated or bored when required to evaluate evidence of a positive nature about the subject.

There may have been a time in history when a belief that slavery was a beneficent institution was epistemically warranted. This was not true of the antebellum south, however. Even if it were the case that slaveholders genuinely *believed* that slavery was paternalistic, it does not follow that it *was* paternalistic. Historians must separate mere rationalizations and gross self-deception from reality.

But, as noted above, some who have explained slavery by using a paternalistic model go beyond making dubious assumptions about the motives of slaveholders; they also present questionable characterizations of slaves. One popular representation under such models is the slave as a totally dependent being. According to this conception, slaves were dependent upon slaveholders because, for a variety of reasons, they could not be responsible for defining and promoting their own good. This argument does not rest on the motives of the slaveholders; the contention could be true even if all slaveholders were motivated to hold slaves because they felt that it would promote their own good rather than the good of the slaves.

Many of the early supporters of this model blatantly assumed the natural inferiority of slaves. Slaves were thought to be subhuman creatures who could not survive in civilized societies if left to their own devices. But what about defenders of the paternalistic argument who denied the natural inferiority of slaves and focused on the so-called lack of autonomy of slaves? Do they fare any better? (This question will be the central issue in the next section of this chapter.)

Liberal thinkers in both the human rights and utilitarian traditions have argued that under certain conditions we are justified in making choices for certain actors even when those choices and the actions that result have consequences that primarily affect the actors themselves. Children, women, blacks, and those who have been thought to have arrested development are among those singled out for paternalistic interference with their liberty. Utilitarians would justify this on the ground that it maximizes utility for society as a whole. Human rights theorists emphasize the importance of protecting human beings from self-inflicted harm.

There can be no denying that there can be praiseworthy motives given for paternalistic interference. There can also, however, be morally reprehensible ones. For example, paternalistic interference can be used by some members of society to justify taking unfair advantage of others under the guise that their actions are protecting the unwilling victims from self-inflicted harm.

I am not the first person to condemn paternalistic explanations or justifications of slavery, and understandably other critics have focused on a controversial premise in paternalistic accounts: namely, that blacks were in some way(s) incapable of recognizing their own good and that slave masters were in a better position to do so. Usually this premise involves some claim about the natural inferiority of blacks or that blacks were made inferior by their social circumstances. But most of these commentators failed to notice that inferiority is a relative term. The judgment that someone is inferior requires a standard of excellence or normality.

During slavery, a common belief held by whites was that blacks were intellectually inferior to whites. Even if the claim were true, however, this would certainly not justify paternalistic explanations and justifications of American chattel slavery. In order for such an account to be viable, it cannot simply be true that blacks were intellectually inferior to whites, but it must further be the case that blacks lacked the mental capacity to understand and promote their own good. So the paternalistic account depends upon blacks failing to reach minimal requirements for autonomous choice. But this claim seems to be clearly false about slaves as a group. Slaves were clearly capable of articulating their conceptions of their good, and they fought against incredible odds to put their life plans into action.[15]

What then should we make of these paternalistic accounts? How should they be understood? We should note that not all interference with a person's will or liberty counts as paternalistic. A person who prevents me from unknowingly falling down an open elevator shaft has not treated me in a paternalistic fashion. All forms of paternalism require that the interference be explained or justified by reference to the good of the person who is being interfered with, some inability or lack of knowledge on the part of the person who is treated in a paternalistic fashion, and the judgment on the part of the person doing the interfering that they know what is good for this person. These conditions appear to be clear and straightforward. But when we look at the various models that have been advanced as types of paternalistic explanations for slavery we discover that they fail to qualify as clear-cut cases of paternalistic interference. In the next section, I shall examine several models of paternalism and show how they have been used to describe slavery.

Models of Paternalism

There are several models that have been used to illustrate paternalistic behavior. In examining these models, I am not claiming that all interferences that fall under them are justified on grounds of paternalism, but rather that they have been thought to represent what we have defined above as a paternalistic interference. All of the models that I shall examine involve at least two parties. It has been argued, however, that people can act paternalistically toward themselves.[16] Such an account eliminates the appearance of a violation of personal autonomy by others. This presents an interesting problem, but it shall not detain us here, for the slaveholder/slave cases involve more than one person. It will, however, be relevant to what I have to say in the next section.

A fairly exhaustive list of popular models of paternalistic interference includes the parent/child model, the mentally competent/incompetent model, the doctor/patient model, the teacher/student model, and the benevolent dictator/citizen model. Can the slaveholder/slave relationship be subsumed under one of the models of paternalistic interferences listed above? I think that the answer is no. Let us turn directly to the question of whether the slaveholder/slave relationship reduces to or is similar in relevant ways to one of these five models.

The parent/child model is the most common one offered as a clear example of paternalistic interference.[17] In fact, many paternalistic accounts of slavery draw upon the parent/child model. In other words, the slaveholder is viewed as the parent and the slave as the child or childlike. The noted historian Kenneth Stampp draws the analogy in the following way:

The most generous master, so long as he was determined to be a master, could be paternal only toward a fawning dependent; for slavery, by its nature, could never be a relationship between equals. Ideally it was the relationship of parent and child. The slave who had most completely lost his manhood, who lost confidence in himself, who stood before his master with hat in hand, head slightly bent, was the one best suited to receive the favors and affection of a patriarch.

The system was in its essence a process of infantilization and the master used the amiable, irresponsible sambos of tradition, who were the most perfect products of the system, to prove that negroes were a childlike race, needing guidance and protection but inviting paternal love as well.[18]

But if we examine carefully the parent/child model advanced by liberal thinkers like Gerald Dworkin,[19] we discover that the analogy between slaveholder/slave and parent/child breaks down. Dworkin tells us that parents' behavior toward their children is thought to be paternalistic because parents force children to do what the parent believes to be in the child's best interest.

The analogy between the parent/child and slaveholder/slave breaks down because the slaves were not all children. But certainly the supporters of this analogy recognize this. So they don't contend that the slaves were children in a chronological sense, but that they were child-like in many important respects. Many thoughtful historians, however, drawing on various sources including the slaves' own narratives, have concluded that attempts to depict adult slaves as "Sambos" or childlike are unfounded. Since slaves were responsible adults who were forced under threat of harm to do the will of another, they cannot accurately be described as children or childlike.

But even if the adult slaves were childlike, the analogy still fails. In the parent/child model, the children will mature and come to see that it was reasonable or unreasonable for their parents to force them, for example, to brush their teeth. The slave-as-child model keeps the slaves as perpetual children. The slaves never mature and never appreciate the reasonableness of the slaveholders' interferences.

If we view the slaves as perpetually childlike, then we move to another model. The competent/incompetent model comes to mind.[20] On this account, slaves are thought to be incapable of determining their own good and choosing the means to achieve it. We should be careful to note that this view does not commit one to the position that slaves were not human beings and thus lacking membership in the moral community. This model includes slaves in the moral community and, as Genovese writes, it insists "upon mutual obligations—duties, responsibilities, and ultimately even rights."[21]

By including slaves in the moral community, however, this model assigns them a moral status—something that was called into question by the very practice of slavery. This account recognizes their humanity or personhood, but what is given with one hand is effectively taken away with the other. Slaves are said to be persons, but they are denied a fundamental feature of personhood; persons should not be used simply as means to the ends of others.

Perhaps I can clarify this point by focusing on how those who are thought to be mentally incompetent have been treated in our society. In brief, the treatment of those who have been characterized as mentally retarded has often been morally reprehensible. Once they were locked away in substandard institutions with little effort being made to see if they could live in mainstream society. Even today far too little is done to determine to what extent these people are capable of shaping and carrying out their own life plans. Very often people designated as retarded were denied what we perceive to be the most basic liberties guaranteed to adult free persons, such as the freedom to enter into sexual relationships. Very often paternalistic reasons were advanced in support of these practices, in spite of the protests of those who were the subjects of these interferences.

What is most interesting about these practices by agents of the state and the medical establishment was that there was often an outright refusal to examine the design of the existing institutions to see if they could be altered or replaced by other institutions that promoted the interests of this group without depriving developmentally disabled citizens of their basic liberties. The tendency was to focus on the individual instead of questioning the existing practices and institutions. The same is true of slavery. It is now clear that this social institution could have been abandoned. This would have allowed blacks to enjoy basic liberties. Of course, this would have altered the holdings of those who benefited from the practice of slavery. But should a just society not be willing to do this if it guaranteed basic liberties to all? The philosopher Rawls thinks so, and I wholeheartedly agree.[22] But how specifically do these remarks relate to the competent/incompetent model as it relates to slavery?

Slaves were not genetically or naturally incompetent. Furthermore, competence is a matter of judgment. It is a socially constructed concept. A person who may be competent in one society may be judged totally incompetent in another. Slaves were made to appear to be incompetent because of the laws, practices, and public opinion of the antebellum South. Slave narratives clearly indicate that even under the most adverse circumstance slaves were able do the things that we think characterize competent adults. So the competent/incompetent model does not apply to slavery.

The teacher/student model may seem to be identical to the competent/incompetent model, but it is not. The student is thought to be uneducated, not incompetent. In the liberal tradition, students are coerced to do things that will enhance their learning because it is felt that doing so promotes their own good. Is the teacher/student model analogous to the slaveholder/slave relationship? I think not.

Some slaveholders did contend that slaves in their natural state were heathens, that it was their duty to educate them in Christian ways, and that slavery was necessary in order to do this. The crucial term here is the necessity of slavery to educate slaves. Clearly there were less coercive and morally acceptable means for converting slaves to Christianity. But let us suppose that there were not more appropriate means available for educating newly acquired adult slaves. This still would not justify the American chattel-slavery practice of keeping the children of slaves and their children enslaved.

What about the doctor/patient model?[23] Can the slaveholder be thought of as the doctor or professional and the slave as his patient or client? I think not. What is crucial in this model is the idea that the patient has chosen to be treated by the doctor. The idea of explicit consent, implied consent, or tacit consent by the patient is thought to justify the doctor's substituting his or her judgment for the judgment of the patient. The question then becomes: has the slave given consent in one of these ways to justify the substitution of the slaveholder's judgment for the slave's on matters of great importance in the slave's life?

It is clear that the relationship between slave and slaveholder was not voluntary. But not all doctor/patient relationships are clearly voluntary. What about emergency situations, where doctors care for patients without their consent? Is the slaveholder/slave relationship like these cases? I think not. In these cases doctors proceed because consent cannot be given. The patient is either unconscious or in some unconscious-like state. But when the patient regains consciousness, he or she certainly has the right to elect to change doctors and in some cases even to refuse medical attention. Again, the slaveholder/slave situation is not like these cases. The slave was never given the opportunity to sever the relationship with the slaveholder.

The doctor/patient relationship that results from emergency situations comes about because there are no other viable alternatives. The slaveholder could claim that if he didn't care for the slaves by substituting his judgment for theirs, the slaves would experience death or great misfortune. But if this were so, it was only because of the institution of slavery (an institution slaveholders created and controlled), and not because of some physical or mental incapacity of the slaves. The slaveholder, unlike the doctor, had other viable alternatives.

What about the final variation: the benevolent dictator/citizen model? Is the slaveholder/slave relationship analogous to this? Let me say first that there is real doubt about whether such a model should be thought of as paternalistic. In order to make the benevolent dictator/citizen

model paternalistic, we must note that the dictator's motive for man-
dating the policies and laws that he does is the promotion of the good
of his citizens. It is not done for personal gain, although personal gain
could be a consequence of the dictator's action. We must further add
that there is some reason to think that the citizens are not able to
recognize and promote their own good. The most controversial assumption, however, is that the dictatorship is preferable on utilitarian
grounds to other forms of government, including democracy. In adding this condition, we assume that the liberty to decide who will gov-
ern and how is not so weighty that it will override the advantages
gained by being subjected to the will of the benevolent dictator.

The model, explained in this way, is paternalistic because it judges
the good of the citizens in strict utilitarian terms. I think there is real
room for doubt about whether this case is in fact paternalistic. It seems
not to be paternalistic because it minimizes the importance of personal
autonomy. The benevolent dictator model might be likened to Plato's
Republic. But on my reading of *The Republic,* it would be wrong to
characterize the philosopher-king as forcing the citizens against their
wills to promote their own good. Plato's citizens did not conceive of
themselves in individualistic terms. They did not separate their individual good from the common or communal good. If autonomy is not
weighty or important, then paternalism is not much of an issue. But
the major voices in the paternalistic debate—J. S. Mill, Dworkin, and
Feinberg—think that autonomy is an issue.

Of course, if we say that what is at stake in paternalistic explanations
is not personal autonomy, then this case can count as paternalistic and
so could slavery. But since I think that what is at stake in describing
something as paternalistic is an imposition upon the autonomy of others, I would not label either relationship paternalistic. Thus, if what I
have argued above is true, we have no good reasons for defining slavery as a paternalistic institution.

Slavery, Paternalism, and Liberalism

Paternalistic explanations have frequently been advanced to support
despicable practices in societies that have an allegiance to such things
as individual liberty and human rights. These societies also have a
strong commitment to a conception of justice that gives priority to the

right over the good. The commitment to these ideals in liberal societies is not merely verbal. There is a long tradition in Western societies of appealing to these ideas to condemn or to justify certain practices. Given that this has been and still is the case, why have paternalistic explanations been so pervasive when it comes to explaining or evaluating the condition of oppressed groups, particularly racial groups?

In an interesting essay, Robert J. Cottrol, a law professor and legal historian, claims that "the contradiction of slavery in liberal America helped to fashion the South's paternalistic ideology."[24] By this he means that the South faced a dilemma. How to embrace the liberal view that all men should be equal before the law and yet condone slavery? He believes that this was an especially acute problem in nineteenth-century America because that period was marked by an extension of suffrage to the nonpropertied, the opening of public schools, and the abolition of imprisonment for debt. All of these liberal reforms contributed to an expansion of freedom for white men and a formal egalitarianism in America, including the South.

This attitude of liberalism fueled abolitionist movements; the proslavery response denied the humanity of blacks and created the paternalistic justification for slavery. By the nineteenth century, the eighteenth-century rationalization that slavery must be preserved until some more prudent new social order could be arranged was rejected and replaced by arguments claiming that slavery was beneficial to the slaveholders as well as the slaves.[25] Why was this so?

I contend that a large part of the answer lies in the fact that paternalistic explanations allow people who benefit from the exploitation of others to mask the contradictions in liberal society. They can use and exploit some members of their society without having to admit that these people are being sacrificed or used strictly as means to support the ends of the dominant group.

The utilitarian principle, which could theoretically justify these practices, sticks in the throats of liberals as I have defined them. The utilitarian principle conflicts in a fundamental way with notions that liberals hold dear. Remember, utilitarianism gives priority to the good over the right and this is hard to swallow for liberals who believe that people should be allowed to define and pursue their own accounts of the good constrained by the right.

The problem for those liberals who are either the powerful majority or a strong minority, then, is to explain how they can continue to enjoy the fruits that result from the exploitation of certain groups and still hold on to the beliefs that I have designated as central to their ideology. They do not want to deny the personhood or humanity of the exploited, nor do they wish to endorse the idea that certain human beings can be used solely as a means for the ends of others. So, for these liberals, paternalism is a way of achieving what they want without having to commit themselves to positions that they find unacceptable. When you add to this the difficulty of saying what counts as paternalism and the cultural and ideological bases for judging competence, then the move to paternalism as a way of masking exploitation is quite an effective strategy for rationalizing the status quo.

My critique of liberalism, as it related to slavery, raises an apparent paradox. As I define liberalism, the ideology gives considerable weight to personal autonomy. But when faced with tough choices as it relates to their own real or perceived self-interest, liberals often readily embrace paternalism. Of course, this apparent paradox could be explained merely as a failure of will. I think, however, the matter is much more complex.

It is safe to say that John Rawls and Robert Nozick are both liberals, even though they clearly disagree over what the state has the right to do when it comes to interfering in the affairs of its citizens.[26] Nozick, for example, contends that the just state has no right to tax its citizens to fund programs to care for needy orphans; Rawls, on the other hand, thinks not only that such programs are permissible, but that they are required by correct principles of justice. Both Rawls and Nozick give priority to the right over the good. In other words, they both claim that they are not imposing a conception of the good upon citizens. But both Rawls and Nozick appeal to a conception of "morality" or of the good based upon an assumed definition of personhood. This is something that is characteristic of all liberals who give priority to right.

It follows that deciding who is a person or a rightholder is crucial for the liberal. Unfortunately, giving necessary and sufficient conditions for personhood is no simple matter. We only have to turn to the heated debate over abortion to attest to this fact. Liberals must contend with two questions: "Who are full-fledged persons?" and "Are all full-fledged persons entitled to decide their own fates even at the cost of lowering their own individual life prospects or social utility?" Few liberals have been able to maintain consistency in answering these tough but crucial questions.

Above, I have argued that American chattel slavery was not paternalistic. If one is still unconvinced by my argument, then perhaps the following example will drive the conclusion home. When slavery and its impact on slaves is discussed, the focus is typically on black males. What about black females? Did their experiences not form an important part of the American slavery experience?

Clearly the answer is yes, and critical studies of the role of black women held as slaves attest to this fact. Important works by Angela Davis, Elizabeth Fox-Genovese, Paula Giddings, Darlene Clark Hine, and Deborah White help us understand American chattel slavery and its aftermath by providing us with insightful journeys into the world of female slaves.[27] Since the female experience was no minor part of the overall slave experience, one would expect that any paternalistic argument would cover their experiences as well. I think the case of female slaves cast serious doubt on paternalistic explanations of slavery.

As a number of historians have shown, black women were typically coerced to bear children. These children were frequently taken away and sold to other slaveholders. The consequences of this practice, as slave narratives graphically reveal, were horrendous. Consider the plight of the slave mother Eliza and her children, Emily and Randall. Their story is told in Solomon Northup's narrative *Twelve Years a Slave*. Northup describes the scene in which Emily and Randall are sold away from their mother:

I have seen mothers kissing for the last time the faces of their dead offspring; I have seen them looking down into the grave, as the earth fell with a dull sound upon their coffins, hiding them from their eyes forever; but never have I seen such an exhibition of intense, unmeasured, and unbound grief, as when Eliza was parted from her child. She broke from her place in the line of women, rushing down where Emily was standing, caught her in her arms. The child, sensible of some impending danger, instinctively fastened her hands around her mother's neck, and nestled her little head upon her bosom. Freeman sternly ordered her to be quiet, but she did not heed him. He caught her by the arm and pulled her rudely, but she only clung the closer to child. Then, with a volley of great oaths, he struck her such a heartless blow, that she staggered backwards, and was like to fall. Oh! how piteously then did she beseech and beg and pray that they might not be separated. Why could they not be purchased together? Why not let her have one of her dear children. "Mercy, mercy, master!" she cried, falling on her knees. "Please, master, buy Emily. I can never work any if she is taken from me: I will die." [28]

Northup notes that Eliza never saw or heard of her children again, but she never forgot them.

What explanation could be provided for saying that such a practice was done for the good of females slaves, or for that matter, slaves in general? One could, I suppose, put forth the transparent argument that slave children would be better off because they could not be cared for properly by their natural mothers. But such a reason is obviously unacceptable. The children were sold to other plantations where they were cared for by female slaves. In fact, if this reason were true, it would be a strong reason for not coercing females to bear children. It is not a reason to have them bear children and then have them sold away.

There is a real danger in going to such lengths to put the above behavior in a better light by describing it as paternalism. Of course, it is good to be sympathetic in interpreting a complex institution like slavery, but there is also a difference between sympathy and distortion. Even allowing individuals of good will to have too much freedom to rationalize inhumane actions has negative consequences. We find this today with people who attempt to minimize the horrors of the Holocaust by maintaining that Nazis were self-deceived, and as such not evil persons. In a similar manner, people who claim that slaveholders promoted the interest of slaves are undermining our common understanding of what counts as an evil act or an evil person.

Perhaps we can all agree that a person who knowingly violates the rights of innocent human beings simply for the sake of doing so is evil. But what about those who violate the rights of others in order to gain or profit? In other words, they do not act this way for its own sake, they do so only because it is a means to what they need or desire. Should such people be described as bad or evil? I think so. If the end they seek can be obtained by a means that does not violate the rights of others, then they can be described as evil for not choosing one of these means. In the case of slavery, the evidence shows that slaveholders were aware that there were other ways to make a living. Nonetheless, they chose to enslave Africans because they wanted a higher standard of living without expending the toil that would have made such a way of life possible.

But the supporters of paternalistic explanations of slavery might object that my analysis fails to appreciate that slaveholders, because of the racism of their times, did not "know" that blacks were deserving of the same protections as whites. They might argue that each generation has moral blind spots. Fifty years from now we may come to deplore things that we now accept as perfectly permissible. The blind spots argument seems to be most compelling in cases where the society at large is blind to certain things because of a lack of information about alternative ways of thinking. This was not the case about the issue of slavery. During the nineteenth century, slaveholders were well aware that there were arguments against slavery and forceful arguments against the belief that blacks were not persons. But what about those who suggest that during the nineteenth century there was still enough uncertainty about the moral status of blacks to warrant slaveholders acting as if blacks had no moral rights? Even if this claim were empirically accurate, it would not justify slavery as a paternalistic institution. If there is uncertainty about the moral status of a being, it does not follow that one should act as if the being has no moral status.

In my view, to ignore the evidence and to continue to describe slavery as paternalistic jeopardizes our understanding of what it means to describe behavior as bad or evil. For if we employ the rationalizations that are used to describe slavery as paternalistic, we can use these same devices to put in a better light behavior that most, if not all, would consider reprehensible. We can justify slavery as paternalistic only at the expense of undermining any realistic account of a public morality.

Three.
Resistance and Slavery

HOWARD McGARY

Historians have documented rebellions and revolts by blacks who were held as slaves.[1] There were violent confrontations between blacks and whites as slaves fought to break their bondage. These occurrences were rare, however, and this fact has led some scholars to question the extent and nature of slave resistance. My aim in this chapter is not to list or examine clear-cut cases of resistance by blacks held as slaves, but to argue that there were more subtle forms of resistance that are often overlooked by historians and other scholars interested in the issue of resistance to slavery. Historians who have endorsed what I have labeled subtle forms of resistance count such things as sabotage, disruption, obstruction, noncooperation, ignorance, illness, and the destruction of farm animals and tools as acts of resistance.[2] Other historians, like George Fredrickson, Christopher Lasch, and Lawrence Levine, have claimed that such acts should not qualify as acts of resistance.[3] For them, resistance is an act that requires planned action involving some actual or potential violence. I disagree, but before we can appreciate the subtle forms of defiance as genuine acts of resistance, we must be clear about what we mean by the concept "resistance."

In the narrative of Linda Brent, a North Carolina slave, we find an interesting account of how the refusal of women slaves to submit to sexual advances of the slaveholder can be seen as resistance to slavery.[4] Elsewhere, we find the refusal by slave women to bear children offered as a form of resistance.[5] According to some definitions, these actions cannot qualify as acts of resistance, but the account of resistance that I construct in this chapter will allow us to include these acts.

There is a voluminous body of literature devoted to chattel slavery in the United States. Some of this literature focuses on the institution of slavery itself, while some focuses on the impact of the American slave system on slaves. In his controversial book *Slavery,* Stanley Elkins compares the American slave system to the Nazi concentration camps. He concludes by argument from analogy that the American slave system broke down the slave's adult personality and reduced him or her to a state of infantile dependency, a state similar to the condition of prisoners of Nazi concentration camps. Elkins calls this personality type a "Sambo." He concludes that one of the tests for the non-Sambo personality is resistance. According to Elkins, the lack of resistance by slaves is evidence that they were "Sambos."[6]

Even prior to Elkins's work, some scholars asserted that black slaves in America were docile and content, concluding that they did not resist slavery.[7] Others have argued strongly against this depiction of the American slave personality and the contention that slaves as a group did not resist slavery.[8]

From a careful reading of the arguments on both sides of the debate, one comes away convinced of the need for clarity concerning how to determine what constitutes "resistance." Merely pointing out instances where slaves acted in docile or aggressive ways does not settle whether such acts constitute acts of resistance. As I have noted, when some historians use the term "resistance" in relation to the actions of American slaves, they have counted a wide range of actions. These actions range from violent direct action against the slave system to slaves avoiding work by pretending to be sick.[9] If scholars are to correctly assess whether American slaves resisted slavery, or for that matter whether any oppressed group resisted its oppression, they first must be able to distinguish resistance from other distinct, but related notions, such as weak compliance.

An examination of resistance could be conceptual in nature or it could focus on actual methods and tactics employed by resisters. I shall not be concerned here with arguing for methods or tactics of resistance, but rather with determining how a third party evaluates whether a person is resisting. Toward this end, I shall raise objections to Roger Gottlieb's groundbreaking essay, "The Concept of Resistance: Jewish Resistance during the Holocaust,"[10] and then offer an alternative account of how we should evaluate whether a person is resisting. I will make use of examples and insights from the long period of slavery in America as well as examples from the civil rights movement.

Gottlieb teases out his account of resistance by focusing on Jewish resistance during the Holocaust. As we will see in the first section, Gottlieb's analysis centers on the beliefs of Holocaust victims about the reduction of their oppression—and by oppression he obviously means to "press down" or to harm. But the better description of the experiences of the victims of the Holocaust is genocide. The aim of the Nazis was not to subjugate Jews, but to eliminate them. In the case of slavery, however, slaves were an important part of the economy of the South and as such they were seen as necessary. So the aims of the Nazis were quite different from the aims of the slaveholders.[11]

Gottlieb's focus on beliefs and intentions is understandable given that he is concerned with an event that is part of fairly recent history. Some Holocaust victims are still alive and can be consulted about their beliefs about resistance to Nazi oppression in concentration camps. This is not the case with slavery. There are no living ex-slaves who can be consulted about day-to-day resistance to slavery.

If any action is to count as a paradigm case of resistance, it would have to be a slave revolt. But even here we discover that our intuitions may differ about what makes it a clear case of resistance. Do we want to count foolhardy self-sacrifice as a case of resistance? If not, why not? We also need to know to what extent a person's actions must be planned or organized in order to qualify as resistance. For example, suppose the slavemaster attempted to march a group of slaves along a road and one person refused to go. He is warned once and then shot dead. Was his action an act of resistance? Does it matter that the person's action has little or no chance of reducing oppression? An adequate account of resistance should answer these questions.

The point of this discussion is not to prove that we can always give a correct judgment about whether certain acts constitute resistance, but to explore different conceptions of how we determine acts of resistance in order to see how they compare with one another, and to discover the consequences of adopting one criterion rather than another as an official account.

Gottlieb on Resistance

Scholars have offered a variety of reasons for why slavery lasted so long. Some incorrectly concluded that its longevity was due in part to a failure on the part of blacks to resist their oppression. Not only do these scholars indulge in blaming the victim; they also fail to appreciate the character of certain actions because of unclarity about the criteria for judging acts of resistance. Those who blame the victims fail to appreciate the destruction of farm tools, suicides, and the "Sambo" personality[12] as genuine acts of resistance. I hope to illustrate that actions and omissions such as these are erroneously seen as acts of contentment, weakness, and even compliance because of a failure by some historians to appreciate how these acts functioned within the slave system.

Philosophers and scholars from other disciplines have examined concepts like oppression, justice, and civil disobedience. Oddly enough, few analytic philosophers have analyzed the concept of resistance. Perhaps this is due to the fact that much of the literature on the topic has been descriptive rather than conceptual in nature. Because of this, philosophers may believe that an examination of questions concerning resistance is empirical and therefore best answered by inquirers from other fields.

Gottlieb is an exception. He contends that, unlike "the concepts of freedom, equality, political rights, and civil disobedience, the concept of resistance has not been analyzed in a manner to help us distinguish acts of resistance from those of passivity, compliance or collaboration."[13] In order to remedy this shortcoming, he concentrates on the state of mind of the person thought to be resisting, rather than the effects of the person's actions. This general strategy is not novel; it has been used to examine other concepts. We find it employed by some legal philosophers in their accounts of the notion of an attempt in criminal law. My examination of the criteria for determining acts of resistance will involve raising fundamental objections both to Gottlieb's conditions for describing an act as one of resistance, and to his general strategy.

A clear account of resistance would be of great value. Not only would it enable us to distinguish resistance from passivity and compliance, it would also help us to judge the legitimacy of the use of force by the state and other bodies. Such an account would also help us to distinguish politically significant acts from mere crimes. For example, we would be in a better position to determine whether blacks and whites who revolted in Watts, Detroit, Newark, and Miami in the 1960s were resisting racial oppression or merely looting and committing assault.

Further, it would allow one to determine whether persons who work within an unjust system can ever be said to be resisting the evils of that system. Finally, if an action can be correctly described as an act of resistance, then this might influence the general population to have sympathy rather than contempt for those committing these acts.[14]

Gottlieb's account of resistance depends upon an account of intentional action. According to Gottlieb, the essential features for an action A to count as an act of resistance are as follows:

(a) Agent S is oppressed and S believes that he or she is oppressed;

(b) S intentionally does A and,

(c) S's intention in doing A involves two sorts of beliefs: (i) S believes that a part of him or her can be threatened, dominated or destroyed by the oppressive relationship, and (ii) S also has beliefs about how the oppressor is exercising the assault or domination, and

(d) either S believed that his or her doing A would directly reduce oppression or S believed that his or her intentionally doing A would set in motion those things that reduce oppression, and

(e) S's belief and desires caused S to do A.[15]

According to Gottlieb's account, if a person genuinely believes that he or she wants to reduce oppression and acts on that belief, then resistance is a correct description of that action even if it is impossible for the action to reduce oppression.

Note that we can separate the question "What makes an act intentional?" from the question, "What makes an intentional act an act of resistance?" My focus will be on the latter.

Gottlieb's account of resistance will not allow us to distinguish paradigm cases of resistance from: intransigence, where people strongly believe that they are resisting but they are not (e.g., a case where a slave's defiance is a personal strategy for self-gratification rather than an action that is intended to reduce oppression); cases of ineffectual resistance (like the slave's mistreatment of farm animals); and cases where one does not believe that one's action constitutes resistance, although functionally it reduces oppression (e.g., an "insider" subverts an unjust government because of agreement with the resistance, but feels that his actions are too insignificant to qualify as acts of resistance).

On Gottlieb's account, we cannot disqualify an act as resistance simply because it is nonaggressive or nonmilitant. Depending upon the person's intention, an extremely ineffective act could count as genuine resistance. For example, during the period of chattel slavery in this country some slaves were assigned jobs as slavedrivers.[16] Their function was to keep other slaves in line. Some of the slavedrivers rationalized their actions by claiming that their intent was to minimize the suffering of slaves, and thus they were reducing oppression. On Gottlieb's account, if their explanations were correct, they resisted, but in an ineffective way.

According to Gottlieb, the goal of an act of resistance must be to lessen oppression, not just to shift its effect or spread it around.[17] But given his condition (d), the agent can adopt quite unrealistic means for achieving his or her goal. Since Gottlieb's account rests on the beliefs of the agent, we must be able to verify the agent's beliefs, especially in odd cases like that of the slavedrivers. On Gottlieb's account, an observer must know the motives of S in order to correctly judge S's action as resistance, but empirically this is often impossible because mental states are not accessible to the observer.

It is understandable why one might want to focus on beliefs about intentions rather than effects or results; but such an exclusive focus is not acceptable. By concentrating on beliefs and intentions we may be better able to judge normative and descriptive concerns related to resistance, like courage and self-worth, but I do not believe we are better able to distinguish acts of resistance from those that are not. The final test of whether or not an act constitutes resistance should not rest solely on an agent's beliefs about intentions. A person's beliefs can be false even though they are firmly held.

Defining acts of resistance in terms of the beliefs of the agent allows a wide range of ineffectual acts to count as acts of resistance. It is important to recognize that it is one thing to define acts of resistance in terms of the agent's intentions and another to determine whether or not the agent has such intentions. Gottlieb's account of resistance places emphasis on intentions. Although he recognizes that the factual question bears on whether we may describe a person's action as resistance, Gottlieb does not give an adequate account of how we can settle whether or not the person has such intentions. Even if he is right that intent is a logically necessary condition for resistance, it is not sufficient for others to establish that a person is resisting.

Gottlieb gives further support for his focus on intention in two sub-sections of his paper, "Tacit Resistance" and "Unconscious or Self-Deceptive Non-Resistance." He claims that with some acts of resistance the beliefs and intentions that the agent has about reducing oppression are tacitly held. The person resists in such cases because of feelings of hatred or guilt rather than an intention to reduce oppression.[18] For Gottlieb these tacit beliefs not only imply that the person has the proper mental state, but that this mental state functioned as motivation for the act of resistance.

Such a reply does not meet my objection, however, although it does explain why unconscious beliefs, in some cases, can give us reason to think that an action is intentional. But it does not explain why we do not need a criterion for determining when a person has certain intentions and if these intentions led to the action in question.

Conscious and Unconscious Resistance

There is an odd ring to the phrase "unconscious resistance." It is puzzling because resistance, like protest, is thought to be a conscious moral and political action, or to at least have a significant moral and political component. As Gottlieb points out, we do make judgments about the actions and characters of persons by virtue of their responses to such things as injustice or oppression. We would certainly like to think, in cases where such character judgments are made, that the actions which form the basis for our judgments are voluntary. In other words, we require that the agent's responses be intentional. If their actions are not intentional, we are inclined to conclude that the unjust or oppressive actions do not reflect on their characters save insofar as their unintentional actions are due to ignorance of things that they should have known about, such as ignorance of the fact that throwing a bomb into a crowded legislative chamber will cause harm to the persons assembled there.

Yet Gottlieb needs something like a concept of "unconscious resistance" if his account is to succeed. He wants to describe certain acts as acts of resistance that, on first glance, appear not to be. He cites some of the nonmilitant and nonaggressive actions of Jews in Nazi concentration camps as resistance because these Jews were either consciously or unconsciously attempting to hold on to their humanity.

This, in the context of Nazi concentration camps, constitutes intentional covert opposition to the oppressor and oppression. On the other hand, Gottlieb dismisses the efforts of the council of influential Jews (*Judenrats*) who appeared to cooperate with the Nazis and administered the Jewish ghettos created by the Nazis. Gottlieb denies that these councils were thereby resisting the Nazi oppression.

Gottlieb incorrectly assumes that cooperation with the oppressor is incompatible with intentionally reducing oppression. This general assumption is clearly false. Persons involved in counterintelligence activities often intentionally cooperate with an oppressive regime in order to eventually halt or reduce its damaging effects. When Gottlieb says that people often have the unconscious aim of reducing oppression, this casts doubt on his rejection of the actions of the *Judenrats* as resistance. The causal relationship in Gottlieb's account disallows accepting effective actions not caused by intent to resist (not just any intent to act).

In the case of unconscious resistance, the action that is done with an unconscious intent to resist is like effective acts not caused by the intent to resist, since unconsciousness implies that the intent is not presently active and, though potentially motivating, it is not presently functioning as a motivator. Put another way, counting unconscious intent is like counting an "almost" in horseshoes: the intent is near the action but not truly connected. True causal connections cannot involve reference to unconscious beliefs.

Gottlieb cannot simply point at the passive or apparent cooperative nature of the *Judenrat's* actions because these could be a part of a chosen strategy to achieve a desired end, namely to reduce oppression by limiting the severity of the punishments inflicted by the Nazis. Perhaps Gottlieb does not focus on the appearance of their actions, but on the actors' beliefs. But if he does, then he must have some satisfactory way of ascertaining whether or not the *Judenrats* had the appropriate intentions. If not, we are allowed to read our own beliefs into what the agent intended when he or she acted. This would violate condition (c) of his account of acts of resistance, which requires the agent to have certain beliefs about thwarting oppression, but does not require the beliefs to be true. Beliefs held with a great deal of conviction can be false or completely out of line with the beliefs of others in the community.

Gottlieb recognizes that beliefs and intentions are problematic criteria, but given his chosen strategy, he must employ them. He asserts that if we encounter entities who appear to be language speakers, but whose sentences translate into beliefs radically different from our own, we might revise our judgment that they were speaking a language. In an analogous fashion, he concludes that if a person's purported beliefs about how to resist in a given situation sufficiently differ from our own, we are justified in believing that this person does not intend to resist.[19]

I disagree. I doubt that we are justified in concluding, on the basis of Gottlieb's account, that a person did not resist. We are only justified in concluding that we have insufficient evidence as to what the person did and why, and thus that we have insufficient information to claim that he or she resisted. For an observer to correctly judge that an action is an act of resistance, it is not necessary for him to know the actor's intentions, or the exact effects of his action.

During the civil rights movement a number of Americans of good will, both black and white, pondered what they should do to reduce the oppression and discrimination experienced by black Americans. Some people adopted a strategy of direct confrontation with unjust governmental practices, including armed self-defense, sit-ins, and attempts to integrate schools, transportation systems, and places of public accommodation. Others used more subtle means, like public lectures exposing the evils of racism, to break down biased racial attitudes; some resolved to build defense mechanisms within themselves to enable them to tolerate oppression. Many of these same tactics were employed by blacks and whites during the antebellum period.

What their actions must all have in common if they are to qualify as acts of resistance on Gottlieb's model, however, is the intent to reduce the oppression of black people. Gottlieb assumes that if S intentionally acts to reduce oppression, then S has a general conception of oppression, but S must also have a specific conception of the particular oppressive system or practice. In the example of the civil rights movement, S must have some knowledge of the Jim Crow system and what is evil and unjust about it. To have the concept of oppression is different from having the concept of "tallness." One can understand what it is to be tall without being committed to any negative evaluative or normative stance, but this is not so with oppression. When one identifies someone's actions or a practice as oppressive, then one is also saying that person's actions or the practice is unacceptable.

Of course, it is debatable whether people who employed very subtle means intended to reduce oppression, but we can attempt to assess their intentions and their sincerity or dedication by determining whether their beliefs about what they intended to do to reduce oppression are consistent with their other beliefs. This will not, however, settle the question, "Are they resisting?" In such cases the person who is said to be intending to resist oppression might have to make a radical revision of his basic set of beliefs.

For example, some students who joined the Student Nonviolent Co-ordinating Committee in its militant but peaceful protest in the South willingly absorbed the violence directed toward the nonviolent protestors. Yet these students categorically rejected Martin Luther King's views on nonviolence.[20] Were their beliefs about why they were engaging in these nonviolent protests consistent with their other beliefs? In all cases I think not. Their actions could not be consistently described as "nonviolent protest" given their beliefs about self-respect and the nature of protest. One might conclude that the students felt the time for self-defensive violence had not yet come and that nonviolence for now was the most effective type of resistance. Such an explanation might explain the actions of some, but not of those who categorically rejected the willing acceptance of violence at the hands of the oppressor. From the fact that a belief B is inconsistent with a person's basic beliefs, it would be deductively invalid to infer that he or she does not have belief B. We lack a failproof method for ascertaining the sincerity of a person's beliefs. This is why we focus on people's actions in order to get some evidence or assurance that their beliefs are, in fact, sincere.

What Gottlieb fails to fully appreciate is the fact that people can believe things that are false, but even more important they can intend to do what is impossible.[21] People with a great deal of sincerity can intend to reduce oppression by adopting such methods as wishing it away or calling on the spirits, and thus count their acts as acts of resistance. If I am right about this, Gottlieb needs a method for ascertaining the sincerity of the agent's beliefs and intentions. His proposal of disqualifying a person's beliefs because they are "radically different from our own" will not suffice. Gottlieb's account fails to provide adequate provisions for consistency and sincerity of belief. His assumption about the superiority of our way of thinking may be classist, racist, or sexist.

Gottlieb is right, however, that we would not do any better by simply focusing on the effects of the agent's action. For instance, during the Watts Riot of 1965 a number of persons engaged in rash, but understandable, actions (such as burning down needed facilities in their communities). They acted with the best of intentions, but the effects of their actions in the short run heightened oppression in Watts rather than reducing it. Denying the reliance on the effects of an action does raise questions about the scope of those who are affected by the reduction of oppression and about how far into the future we should look if we are to employ an analysis which examines effects. If we focus only on the short-term effects of actions and limit the scope to blacks in the Watts community, we would certainly conclude that they did not resist. Gottlieb fails to see that what is crucial when a third party determines whether an action counts as an act of resistance is not always what the agent actually believes and intends, but the circumstances the agent faced at the time of action.

In civil law a person can be justifiably held liable for an action he did not intend to commit and for consequences he did not expect. For example, in Re Polemis and Furness, Withey and Co. (3KB 560 [1921]), stevedores in the employ of Furness, Withey and Company knowingly carried planks near the hatch of a ship that their employer had chartered. They inadvertently dropped a plank into the hold, creating a spark and a fire because, unbeknownst to them, kerosene had been stored there and some gaseous fumes were still in the hold. The court ruled that Furness, Withey and Company were liable even though there was no intention to cause the fire or reason for the stevedores to anticipate that a fire would result from dropping a plank into the hold.

In a like manner, persons can be correctly said to have resisted oppression even though we lack reliable information about their beliefs or intentions when they acted. I believe that we may justifiably conclude that the slaves' practice of stealing from their masters was a form of resistance even though we do not have reliable information about what their actual intentions were when they stole or about the actual consequences of their acts on the slave system. The evidence for this interpretation is supported by the fact that slaves stole from slaveholders at great risk to themselves even when their survival needs were met. Orlando Patterson has argued that stealing by slaves was a way for them to assert their humanity.[22] I would add it was a way of resisting the oppressive characterization of themselves as nonpersons.

Even in the absence of open rebellion or evidence of a worked-out plan for resisting slavery, I believe we are warranted in concluding that stealing by slaves from their masters, under certain circumstances, counts as "day-to-day" resistance to slavery. These acts, in the context of slavery, can reasonably be seen as efforts to reduce oppression by frustrating the demands of the slave system. I disagree with those historians who claim that only the testimony of slaves themselves can tell us whether they resisted slavery.

If historians, sociologists, and other analysts are really to develop adequate criteria to distinguish acts of resistance from those that are not, they should not always give primacy to an agent's intentions. They should focus on the conditions that the agent faced when he or she acted or failed to act and the avenues available for reducing oppression. With this information, a better strategy to adopt in order to distinguish acts of resistance from those that are not would be one similar to the reasonable person test in the law. The reasonable person test denotes a hypothetical individual who possesses and exercises those qualities of attention, knowledge, intelligence, and judgment which a decent society requires of its members for the protection of their interests and the interests of others. A person's intentions and their effects are sometimes useful, but they are not always necessary in order to make a judgment about whether the act is an act of resistance.

One of my central points is to question how we assess the existence of an intent, a belief, and their connection to an action. Intents and beliefs are mental states, and hence not directly observable by a third party. At times they may not even be observable by the agent (we do not always know the causes of our actions). The reasonable person hypothesis seems to offer a workable solution. But the question remains: "Reasonable in what sense?" A solution may be formally reasonable or pragmatically reasonable. The former is theoretically elegant, but in practice it may be ineffective. The latter is relativistic, and thus we need greater detail of its operation if it is to prove helpful.

"Reasonable" in the context of the legal test is a culture-bound concept. It refers to the consensus of persons in the culture. My test for resistance will also be culture-bound, but this is as it should be. I should note that my account of how we determine whether or not an act counts as resistance recognizes the existence of belief and intent, but, as I have suggested, my mechanism differs from Gottlieb's because it does not depend upon assessing the sincerity of each. My account of resistance cannot tell us that resistance, in fact, has occurred, but only that it is likely that it did. When you deal in the empirical and practical, absolutes are often unattainable.

It might seem counterintuitive to accept an account of resistance that does not require the resister to intend to reduce oppression. But this is because we mistakenly believe that it is redundant to say that S intentionally resisted his oppressors. When we think of someone resisting, we assume that they intended their action to reduce oppression or set in motion those things that will lead to the reduction or the elimination of oppression. I believe, however, that we need to distinguish: (i) S intended to do A from (ii) S did A and S's action was intentional.

We should not assume that a correct analysis of how a third party identifies an act of resistance should have (i) as a necessary condition. We often perform an *action* intentionally with no intention of bringing about an important and reasonable *description* of that action. For example, one may intentionally eat sweets with no intention of ingesting food with a high caloric content. The actions of very young children can sometimes be correctly described as acts of resistance even though these children did not, under a description of their actions, have an intention to reduce what they perceived to be oppression.

In fact, in some cases of resistance the resisters have no clear conception that they are being oppressed. This is true with young children who have not formed a clear general conception of oppression, but it is also true of persons who have a clear conception of oppression in general terms but lack a full understanding of the particular nature of the oppression that they are experiencing. Such cases are graphically illustrated by examples drawn from the oppression of women. Housewives intentionally engage in actions that under an appropriate description can be said to reduce their oppression without having intended to do so under their own description of their actions.

Gottlieb wants to handle such cases by claiming that these women unconsciously intend to reduce their oppression. I think this assumes that certain beliefs are present in the mind, but that they have not yet been brought to the surface. I contend that there need not be such unconscious beliefs in such cases. A desire to ease a feeling of dissatisfaction is not always something that can be turned into beliefs about the specific nature of one's oppression and how to reduce it, even with a great deal of effort devoted to consciousness-raising.

It is my contention that many acts of resistance lacked the *mens rea* condition because they were behavior patterns that were passed down from generation to generation, having the consequence of reducing oppression or force without the resister having conscious or unconscious beliefs about the reduction of some force or oppression. Perhaps those slaves who originated the practice had the intention of reducing oppression by engaging in the acts that established it. For strategic reasons, they may have chosen to teach these practices to their children as routine behaviors.[23] This would have the effect of keeping the practices clandestine since even if slaves who acted in these ways were interrogated by the slaveholders, they could not reveal any intentions about reducing oppression because they did not have them.

Remember, on my account, the agent's beliefs are sufficient, but not necessary. Given that chattel slavery in the United States lasted so long and that the system had clearly established procedures for keeping slaves in check, it is not surprising to find that resistance took this form.

An Alternative Account of Resistance

If the above observations are correct, then the features of action A that are essential for A to be judged by a third party as an act of resistance should be reformulated as follows:

(a)' The condition of constraint (positive or negative) exists against agent S and the group in which S is a member, and S has a general conception of these constraints, and

(b)' S's action A is intentional under S's description of A which may or may not be the same description under which S's action A reduces the constraint, and

(c)' S's action A under an appropriate description is one that could reduce the constraint directed at the group of which S is a member, and

(d)' The causal process that S sets in motion with his action A is one that reasonable persons, who are similarly constrained and aware of their constraints, would also be likely to set in motion if they wanted to reduce these constrictions.

In the discussion above, I did not challenge Gottlieb's focus on oppression as the object of the resistance. But condition (a)' reflects my disagreement with Gottlieb's contention that resistance is always resistance to oppression. We can resist things that are not oppressive, even in the political context. By adopting the above conditions, we are still able to preserve an important feature of the act of resistance, namely the moral importance attached to an act that reduces oppression. At the same time, we avoid the difficulties raised to Gottlieb's account of resistance, because S can engage in an action that causally reduces or sets in motion those acts that will reduce oppression even though, at the time he or she acted, S may not have intended to reduce oppression.

From the point of view of a historian, this account of when a person can be said to have resisted focuses on the moral import of the action rather than the person. It does not attempt to identify the state of mind of the actor but rather focuses on the fact that the agent acted and that his action was judged from the perspective of the oppressed to be an important part of a causal process that could reasonably lead to the reduction of oppression.

The revised account of when some third party's action can correctly describe an act as resistance avoids counting conformist acts as resistance because the agent believed them to be so. It would not allow us to count as acts of resistance the actions of those slaves who sincerely believed that informing the slave masters of the efforts of fellow slaves would bring down the slave system. Allowing these conformist acts to count as resistance, because the agent intended them to be so, serves to hamper rather than to encourage political efforts to reduce oppression. Counting such actions as resistance allows too much room for misguided persons to self-deceptively ease their consciences by erroneously concluding that they had contributed to the reduction of oppression.[24]

It may seem that my adoption of the reasonable-person test makes me susceptible to the same criticism that was raised against Gottlieb. In other words, we allow the belief of others to be a substitute for the beliefs of those said to be resisting. This does not present a problem for my account, however, because I do not make the agent's beliefs about the reduction of oppression a necessary condition for describing an act as resistance.

It is incumbent upon me nevertheless to show why my account does not allow the oppressors or supporters of the status quo to use the reasonable-person test to discount legitimate acts of resistance. But remember that the reasonable-person test is culture-bound and, as such, subject to abuse by persons with power and influence. Therefore I would argue that the determination of what counts as resistance must involve a genuine public dialogue, with care taken to empower and acknowledge the voices of those who directly share the legacy of social practice like slavery and the Holocaust.[25]

What my account of resistance highlights is the fact that we should avoid the temptation to tailor our accounts to accommodate only cases of oppression in recent history. On the other hand, we do not want to focus solely on effect simply because there are no survivors who can be interviewed about their beliefs about the reduction of oppression. Hopefully, the account of resistance that I have sketched here suffers from neither of these shortcomings.

This account of resistance appreciates but rejects any account of resistance that makes beliefs about the intent to reduce oppression necessary for the identification of an act of resistance. In order to fully understand the wide range of acts of resistance, however, one must recognize that resistance to certain acts by victims of oppression is not directed at some generic, general condition of oppression, but to specific actions and practices. For example, the action and practices that make up the institution of slavery were not identical with those that define the Holocaust. As noted earlier, the slaveholder wanted to act to make the slave a profitable piece of human property, whereas the intent of the Nazis was the extermination of the Jews.

The means adopted to achieve these different goals may have been similar in certain respects, but there were some important differences. For example, in order to appreciate the refusal to work or the destruction of farm tools by slaves as acts of resistance, one must be knowledgeable about the specific nature of the practices on the plantation and the context in which these acts took place. It is my contention that those who wish to evaluate such actions would be better served in some cases by focusing on what slaves were up against instead of always trying to determine the slaves' actual beliefs about whether their actions were intended to reduce oppression. Remember, my disagreement with Gottlieb is not that the beliefs of slaves are never useful in determining acts of resistance, but rather that such beliefs are not necessary in order to describe an act as resistance.

It is important to note that a primary assault of chattel slavery was the attempt by slaveholders to get slaves to accept or rationalize their miserable predicament. It is clear from reading slave narratives that slaveholders were successful to some degree in achieving this desired result. People who have been indoctrinated from the time of birth to accept oppressive practices and lifestyles very often do not possess even unconscious beliefs about the specific nature of some of the oppressive practices to which they emotionally and physically react.

In fact, as the black liberation movement in the United States and the women's movement have shown us, it is not the case that oppressed people are always knowledgeable about their oppression. Black Americans and women did not always possess beliefs about their oppression. It is doubtful that these beliefs existed in their unconscious mind in the way that the truths of mathematics were said to exist in the mind of the slave boy in Plato's *Meno*, nor were they suppressed in the way Freud described. The victims of certain types of oppression have to learn rather than recollect or cease to suppress their beliefs about oppression.

It is clear why Gottlieb wants to focus on unconscious beliefs. He adopts a Davidsonian account of reasons as causes of action.[26] So, in his mind, in order to say that S resisted W then S must have had certain beliefs which counted as his reasons for acting. For Gottlieb, even in those circumstances where the agent S does not acknowledge the requisite belief about the reduction of oppression, such beliefs have to exist and be operative, even if they exist in S's unconscious mind. As I said earlier, the move to the unconscious mind is crucial for Gottlieb because it allows him to expand the class of acts that can be said to qualify as acts of resistance.

My worry with this approach is that it fails to fully appreciate the far-reaching affects caused by prolonged oppression. Gottlieb assumes that people, for the most part, have a clear picture of what is oppressive in their lives and why. Given that his focus was the Holocaust, his adoption of this model is understandable.

Compared to slavery, the Holocaust lasted a relatively short period of time. Victims knew clearly what it meant to be free persons and what it meant in very specific terms to live a life free of Nazi oppression. Chattel slavery in the United States, on the other hand, lasted for several hundred years. Most slaves never knew what it meant to live lives free of the domination of slaveholders. This fact should not be ignored if one is to develop an adequate account of the role that beliefs about the nature of one's oppression play in my accounts of resistance to slavery.

It is important that we make it clear that my adoption of the reasonable-person test does not commit me to the counterintuitive result whereby a slave's actions count as resistance to slavery even if the slave did not see slavery as oppressive, but actually delighted in its existence. Consider the following hypothetical case:

Imagine the situation, on W^*, where slaves played "the stealing game," the object of which was to see who could steal the most from his or her master without getting caught. These slaves, as it turns out, liked slavery and amused themselves by playing "the stealing game." Now, some slaves who put their hearts into the game exhibited great skill—so much so, that the "stealing game" had a negative impact on W^*'s economy. But, except for the "stealing game," the slaves were otherwise obedient, loyal, and respectful.[27]

Does this case satisfy all of my conditions for resistance and thus serve as a counterexample to my account of resistance? I think not. An important feature of my account is that the person who is said to be resisting is dissatisfied or unhappy with their predicament. But from the fact they are unhappy with or frustrated with their situation, it does not follow that they believe that specific practices that caused their predicaments are oppressive. Unhappiness and frustration accompany oppression, but these states do not entail that one is oppressed or that one believes that one is oppressed.

The American slave experience, given its brutality and longevity, can tell us a great deal about extremely provocative questions concerning the nature of resistance. For example, is it fair to call an act resistance if one believes that the action will be ineffectual or foolish? It is also useful to know if every act of resistance is an act of courage.

Let us now turn to the first of these questions. When we say that an act is foolish, it is most often judged against the prevalent beliefs and standards of the time. Of course, sometimes we say that something is foolish if the action runs counter to what we take to be irrefutable facts, like the laws of nature. But in most instances, the claim that an action is foolish is judged relative to our existing norms and practices. We take these norms and practices to be true, but they are at best only contingently true. My contention is that when we examine the wisdom of most alleged acts of resistance in the case of slavery, we should recognize that what might be foolish or foolhardy for a white free person would not be foolish for a black person caught in the muck of slavery. We should also note that what might be foolish for persons struggling under a certain set of oppressive practices may not be foolish for those struggling under a different set.

These are extremely important questions because, as many commentators on slavery have noted, slavery was an extremely complex institution in economic, psychological, and sociological terms. The relationships that existed between slaves and their owners were multidimensional. For example, slaves were dehumanized by their slaveholders but they were also involved in intimate relationships with them. So, the battle lines between slaves and slaveholders were not as clearly drawn as, say, in war-time situations, where the enemy is distinct and clearly identifiable. This is not to say that the majority of slaves did not see slaveowners as adversaries, but rather that the very nature of chattel slavery clouded some issues and caused slaves to act in ways that they would otherwise not have acted had they controlled their own destinies. When one makes an assessment of the behavior of a slave, one must keep these things in mind and not be too quick to accept what might seem like an obvious interpretation of a slave's behavior.

With consuming and tightly controlled institutions such as slavery, one should not expect each and every act of resistance to be efficacious. Some of the most effective acts of insurrection taken alone would have been judged as foolish or hopeless prior to the time of action. Some actions have a way of motivating other actions, but it is often impossible to predict with any certainty which actions will have this effect. Nonetheless, we still want to be able to distinguish acts by cowards that turn out to have positive results from actions by brave persons who intentionally act to thwart specific oppressive practices.

My account of resistance allows us to make such a distinction because the beliefs of the actor *can* be used as evidence but they *need* not be used. If, for example, a slave wishes to poison a rival for his girl-friend's affections, but inadvertently poisons a notoriously brutal slave overseer, should the slave's act qualify as an act of resistance? It might, and my account of resistance supports my thinking. My account allows us to examine and use the beliefs of the actor when they are readily apparent; when they are not, we can examine the action in its context, in the light of existing norms and practices, in order to make a judg-ment about whether or not the action qualifies as resistance.

In these cases, it might seem that my account completely ignores the motives of the actor in an assessment of the action. This view is mistaken. We make inferences about the agents' motives, but we do not assume that every act that qualifies as an act of resistance was performed by someone with a belief (conscious or unconscious) about the reduction of oppression. So, it is true that we sometimes call an act resistance even though we have to remain silent about such things as the courage of the actor. Is this an unacceptable consequence of my account? I think not.

We often associate acts of resistance with courage, but it would be a mistake to claim that every act of resistance is an act of courage. Aristotle wrote that courage is the proper mixture of fear and cheer.[28] By this he meant that a courageous person takes risk, but not to the point of being foolhardy. However, some risks are greater than others. For example, we all know that extending a pole to a drowning person involves some risk and that the results of such an action are clearly noble, but we would refrain from calling such an action courageous because the risk of harm to the rescuer is so slight. If I am right that courage involves taking risks that can not be described as minor, then clearly some acts of resistance will not qualify as courageous acts. When we are informed about the full range of acts of resistance to slavery, then we will see that in the day-to-day acts of resistance, courage was not always the issue.

Four.
Citizenship and Slavery

BILL LAWSON

O NE OF THE MOST important events of Reconstruction was the rat-
ification of the Fourteenth Amendment to the United States
Constitution.[1] Section One of this Amendment states:

all persons born or naturalized and subject to the jurisdiction thereof are
citizens of the United States and of the state wherein they reside. No state
shall make or enforce any laws which shall abridge the privileges or immunities of citizens of the United States: nor shall any state deprive any
person of life, liberty, or property without due process of law; nor deny
to any person within its jurisdiction the equal protection of the laws.[2]

The importance of this amendment for the political standing of blacks
was cited by Senator Lot M. Morrill of Maine during debate in the
Senate on the legislation:

If there is anything with which the American people are troubled, and if
there is anything with which the American statesman is perplexed and
vexed, it is what to do with the negro, how to define him, what he is in
American Law, and what rights he is entitled to. What shall we do with
the everlasting, inevitable negro? is the question which puzzles all brains
and vexes all statesmen. Now, as a definition, this amendment [to Section
I which establishes the citizenship of the native of African descent] settles
it. Hitherto we have said that he was nondescript in our statutes; he had
no status; he was ubiquitous; he was both man and thing; he was three
fifths of a person for representation and he was a thing for commerce and

for use. In the highest sense, then . . . this bill is important as a definition.[3]

While the adoption of the Fourteenth Amendment may have settled the question of citizenship for blacks in the minds of many legal theorists, there were some black political theorists who still did not see themselves as Americans. They insisted that there is a fundamental incompatibility between what some whites thought America stood for and what it means for blacks who find themselves physically within, but in all significant respects alien to, this polity.

Historically, there have always been people who denied that blacks belonged in America.[4] Even some whites who fought against slavery thought that blacks could not ever become full citizens.[5] In the 1850s, a growing segment of Northern opinion "opposed slavery but resisted the radical abolitionist demand that blacks be accepted after emancipation as a permanent and participating element in American society."[6] There was a consensus among many whites that America had been founded for the white man and that the two races were socially and politically incompatible. Blacks, it was argued, would never achieve equal citizenship status in America.

Many black thinkers agreed that white Americans would never accept blacks as equals. According to these thinkers, blacks could flourish only if they left the United States and established their own country.[7] Prior to emancipation, the United States Supreme Court, with the Dred Scott decision, did nothing to make blacks think that their lowly status in America would change.

Much of the debate by blacks, from the beginning of their presence in America, focused on what to do given the negative treatment of all blacks in America. Proposals on how to respond generally took one of four routes: individual growth, or improvement within the American system by moral suasion (integrationist); universal freedman betterment, or development of political power via separate social institutions; resettlement, or development of separate communities in territories not having slaves; and emigration/colonization, to Liberia, Haiti, elsewhere in the Caribbean, or West Africa.[8]

While these views merit philosophical analysis in their own right, I am concerned with an argument presented by Robert Brock, a political activist and president of the Self-Determination Committee of Los Angeles. His argument can be stated as follows:

(1) blacks came to America by force;

(2) their presence here is not voluntary;

(3) their consent has never been sought;

(4) blacks were even made citizens without their consent;

(5) by not being allowed to choose, blacks were denied the basic rights that would make them real citizens;

(6) failure to get their consent undermines any claim to citizenship; and

(7) therefore, blacks are not citizens[9]

While this argument may appear valid, Harvey Natanson, a philosopher, realizes the importance of closely examining the soundness of such arguments. He argues that citizenship requires consent. He goes on to contend that a careful consideration of consent theory will show that some blacks in the United States were never in a position to consent to the state. These blacks, he concludes, were not legally obligated.[10]

Natanson's position draws on what he takes to be a Lockean model of the democratic state, relying heavily on John Locke's notion of government by consent. According to Locke, individuals incur political obligations by joining with other individuals in a social pact that gives rise to civil society. This pact is called a "social contract." An important aspect of the social contract is the belief that the individuals who form the pact are free, autonomous beings. Their consent to the contract must be freely given. The state should provide more protection than one would receive without a civil government. It almost goes without saying that Locke's political theory has had a powerful influence on American political thought.[11]

According to Natanson, given Locke's influence on American political thought, it is only natural to use Locke's theory of political consent to assess the political situation of blacks in America. He labels this Lockean position the "American-traditional" view of legal obligation.[12] Natanson believes that if we accept the Lockean account, some blacks, because of their unique history, remain in a Lockean "state of nature." The state of nature for Locke was a pre–civil society arrangement, where individuals had only themselves to depend on for the protection of their property. In this state there was no common law, no judge, and no agreed-upon person to punish violations of property rights.

This conclusion is worth examining for several reasons. First, the argument forces us to rethink our understanding of the nature of consent theory as a justification for state membership and political/legal obligation. Such an examination raises the following questions: what impact did being enslaved have on blacks giving political consent? Can we find a sign of black consent during Reconstruction? [13] Second, Natanson's argument is important for evaluating the present legal obligations of blacks. [14] Third, it may help us better to understand Locke's political theory. Fourth, while the Natanson article was written at the apex of the civil rights struggle, the argument that blacks did not consent to become United States citizens has a long history in the African-American community. In fact, it is still articulated by some members of the black community, as a call either for reparations or for the development of a black state. [15]

In what follows, I shall argue against both Natanson's conclusion about the citizenship status of blacks and his reading of Locke. I show that Locke's position, at least in *The Second Treatise,* supports the claim that all black Americans are citizens and, as such, have legal obligations as citizens. I shall also argue that there are no blacks in the United States who are in a Lockean state of nature. Natanson's argument is unsound because: he focuses on the wrong passages in Locke; he shows very little insight into the political history of black Americans; and he neglects the fact that citizenship through birthright is an important aspect of American law. Finally, Locke's work supports the position that the acts of civil disobedience in the 1960s were, in fact, a justifiable and permissible response to the social and political injustices suffered by blacks.

The Social Contract and Blacks

An adequate defense of Natanson's position requires two arguments: first, that at the end of slavery some blacks remained in a state of nature, even after the passage of the Thirteenth and Fourteenth Amendments to the United States Constitution; and second, that there are some present-day blacks who are still in a state of nature. Let us now turn to the claim that some blacks after emancipation and the postwar amendments remained in a state of nature.

Natanson draws on two interrelated arguments from Locke to assess the political status of freed slaves at the end of the Civil War. He begins with the Lockean proviso that human beings have an inalienable right to life, liberty, and estate. This inalienable right existed in the state of nature and should be retained in civil society. Because civil society provides more security, people are quite willing to leave the state of nature and "join in society with others who are already united, or have a mind to unite for the mutual preservation of their lives, liberties and estates."[16]

Unfortunately, Natanson does not tell us what he means by "more security." The right to be protected is remarkably difficult to construe, but we do know that if a person is to be protected, presumably he or she must be protected from something. But what? We can, at least, agree to this: a liberal democratic state must provide protection from such abuses as lynching, assaults, and so forth. In addition, a liberal democratic state must ensure that a citizen be protected from political, legal, and public interferences in the exercise of his or her rights, provided that his or her actions do not violate the rights of others.[17]

Drawing on Locke, Natanson thinks that the state must provide the individual with more security than she or he would have had in the state of nature. Otherwise, there is no need to enter into the contract with other individuals. In the case of many blacks, it is clear that they were not accorded governmental protection as citizens while they were slaves. Blacks at the end of slavery, however, hoped that they would be accorded equal protection under the law. Unfortunately, their high hopes and government actions did not coincide.[18]

If, at emancipation, a pact was supposed to exist between blacks and the government, the government did not live up to its part of the contract. It is clear, according to Natanson, that some blacks never received the protection of their life, liberty, and property as would be mandated if they were citizens of the United States. Because governmental protection was never given, there was no social contract to accept. He thinks that it follows from this that the Negroes in question were not parties to the contract, for it is the acceptance of the governmental protective services which defines membership. According to

Natanson, the government's failure to protect some blacks was not because these blacks did not want protection, but because it was never
offered. As a consequence, these blacks remained in the state of nature.[19]

Consent and Blacks

If the lack of protection were not enough, Natanson also thinks that
Locke's position on consent, which forms the basis for his second argument, also supports the position that some blacks were still in a state
of nature at the end of slavery.

Natanson realizes, however, that the political situation in America is
very different from that Locke envisioned in *The Second Treatise*. He
nevertheless thinks that historically the concept of consent (despite its
weakness) has become important in the American political tradition as
a justification for obedience to the law: the citizen ought to obey the
law because he or she freely chose, by acceptance of government protection, to enter into a contract, one which provides him with a superior service that he or she cannot duplicate in a state of nature.

According to Natanson, when a native-born American joins those
who accept the authority of the government, he or she does not indicate his consent either verbally or in writing, for there are no rites of
entry into the social order. If explicit verbal or written consent is not
given, is there some evidence that indicates that a native-born American acted by free choice and not coercion to become a willing party to
the agreement? For Natanson, it is by acceptance of the most essential
service the government can offer him, superior protection of his natural right to life, liberty, and estate (if we reason in line with the basic
tenets of the natural-rights theory), that the individual expresses free
consent to an agreement or contract with the government. Accepting
government protection constitutes consent in its deepest meaning and
at the same time is an establishment of contract.[20] In other words, to
accept governmental protection willingly is to agree to government itself—in essence, it is an acceptance of genuine citizenship with all its
benefits and responsibilities.

While noting that Locke thinks that only through explicit and expressed consent can a person become a true member of the state, Natanson contends that this is not completely applicable to the American

political scene. In America, agreement to the social contract is made tacitly, by acceptance of government protection of one's natural rights. He admits that his version of tacit consent allows it to be as binding as Locke's expressed consent.

Using this modified version of Locke's position on consent, Natanson assesses the political status of freed slaves. His position here turns on whether or not, when American citizenship was conferred to blacks, they were in a position to give their consent. Natanson believes that politically unprotected blacks had not been in a position to dispose of their possessions and persons as they saw fit because slavery was a condition that severely restricted their personal autonomy. The inability of many blacks to have any control over their person caused many whites to conclude that slaves were children or childlike. Of course, one has to forget here that the behavior of blacks toward whites was impacted by the chattel slavery system.

Nevertheless, because blacks were seen as children or childlike, Natanson thinks that the government of the United States took a paternalistic position regarding citizenship and blacks. Blacks were denied the freedom to make any choice at all. The government thought that blacks were unable to choose and made them citizens without their consent. "Thus, in their involuntary alienation from the American contract, these Negroes have been considered lacking in the potential for self-determination."[21]

If, however, blacks were capable of choosing United States citizenship and were not allowed to do so, they were denied a basic right: "Either way, these blacks were made citizens without their consent or input."[22] What, then, was the political status of those blacks who were made citizens? Natanson claims that they were nonparticipants in the contract, and, as such, not genuine citizens.

These blacks thus had a unique status. According to Natanson, because they were not allowed to freely choose, these blacks are still in a state of nature.[23]

The consideration of social contract thus leads Natanson to two conclusions: first, freed blacks are not genuine citizens; and second, they are still in a state of nature. According to Natanson, blacks must look to themselves for protection of their inalienable rights because the government cannot be counted upon to honor its part of the bargain. It follows, within the framework of the quid-pro-quo justice inherent in the American-traditional view of legal obligations, that "it cannot be held that these excluded Negroes [sic] ought to obey the law."[24]

The State of Nature and Blacks

Let us assume that Natanson is correct about the following things: some blacks were not protected; there is no problem with his version of tacit consent; and his version of consent does bind an individual to the state. First, does it follow that those blacks were left in a state of nature? And second, does it also follow that some present-day blacks are still in a state of nature and not obligated legally to the government of America? The answer to both questions is no, but in order to see why, we need to assess Natanson's assumptions about the legal and moral status of blacks at the end of the Civil War.

Did slavery so undermine the autonomy of blacks that they were not in a position truly to consent to the state? Was slavery the ultimate destroyer of autonomy? Did slavery, as Stanley Elkins claims, render the slave incapable of making an informed decision?[25] Did the United States government fail to provide any assistance for newly freed slaves? What would show that former slaves had freely consented to the state?

It is possible to draw out one scenario to illustrate what needed to be done to ensure that blacks were informed about what it meant to be a citizen of the United States. Imari Obadele, founder and president of the Republic of New Africa, argues that blacks at the end of the Civil War should have been offered four options: become citizens of the United States; be allowed to leave the country; start their own country, either in the United States or some other country; or return to Africa.[26] It was the responsibility of the government to ensure that blacks were informed of their choices and then to provide the funding necessary for them to carry them out.

It must be assumed that, when Natanson claims that some blacks did not freely consent, he means either that at the enactment of the Fourteenth Amendment, some blacks were not in a position to understand what it meant to be citizens or that these blacks were not allowed to choose. Natanson, at times, seems to be making both claims. Either way, he believes, their acceptance of citizenship would not really be consent-based.

This position, however, is not supported by a careful reading of

African-American history, in at least three important ways. First, the debate over the future of blacks in America was not limited to whites. Blacks had discussed the options open to them well before the Emancipation Proclamation. Paul Cuffe, a black businessman and merchant, as early as 1816 paid for the passage of free blacks to Freetown, Sierra Leone.[27]

But some people questioned the value of emigration as a way to solve the black problem. Frederick Douglass criticized all emigration schemes.[28] The general concerns of many blacks were stated in an open letter which Robert Purvis sent to the government emigration agent on August 28, 1862: "The children of the black man have enriched the soil by their tears, and sweat, and blood. Sir we were born here, and here we choose to remain."[29] Most blacks were committed to becoming United States citizens with all of the rights and responsibilities that come with citizenship.

Second, the view of blacks as hopeless victims has been challenged and shown to be false by W. E. B. DuBois, John Blassingame, Eric Foner and others. Their research also demonstrates that slavery was not as morally and intellectually damaging for blacks as had been suggested by Elkins.[30]

Freed slaves behaved responsibly. In South Carolina, for example, there was a generous appraisal of the personnel of a Negro delegation for the way they handled the responsibilities of government. Many of the state constitutions drawn up in 1867 and 1868, authored by blacks, were the most progressive the South had ever known.[31]

Furthermore, the federal government did try to help with the adjustment from slavery to freedom. When the Thirteenth Amendment was passed by Congress, Lincoln supported it; but it was his opinion that the transition from slavery to freedom should be a gradual procedure. After several plans to colonize freed slaves failed, he studied various means of making this transition. He favored a type of apprenticeship such as that tried by Great Britain, also later practiced in Maryland.[32]

In the end, the United States government established the Freedmen's Bureau as a government agency to oversee the social and political incorporation of blacks into the system. The bureau was established by an act of the United States Congress on March 3, 1865, to distribute clothing, food, and fuel to the destitute freedmen and oversee "all subjects" relating to their condition in the South. Despite its unprecedented responsibilities and powers, the bureau was clearly envisioned as a temporary expedient. Incredibly, no budget was appropriated—it would have to draw funds and staff from the War Department.[33]

The greatest impact of the Freedmen's Bureau was in the area of education. Education was not one of the original functions of the bureau but in 1866 became one of its authorized purposes:

By 1869, there were 9,503 teachers in schools for freedmen, with about 5,000 of them from the Northern states. At the beginning, nearly all of the teachers were whites from the North; but in 1870, the bureau reported that there were 1,324 Negro teachers out of a total of 3,300. By 1869, thirteen high schools or colleges had been established. In building the education system, the Freedmen's Bureau made major contributions, while the devoted and dedicated white teachers who came from Northern states were its agents in the schools. Their work was reflected in the noteworthy lives of many thousands of freedmen.[34]

The evidence is clear: the Freedmen's Bureau did have an important impact on the political and educational status of blacks after the Civil War.[35]

The government failed to protect the legal rights of many blacks, however, by withdrawing federal troops from Southern states, by failing to prevent the rise of the Ku Klux Klan, and by the enforcement of Jim Crow laws. Does this failure mean that blacks were no longer citizens? Before we address this question, we should note that blacks were cognizant of their choices; they chose to accept citizenship, and they attempted to make their citizenship real. It was not the unwillingness of blacks which caused the problems that developed around their citizenship, but governmental inaction.

To be specific, the governmental inaction was its failure to continue to ensure that the political power of blacks would not be usurped by the former slaveholders. The government pulled federal troops out of the South soon after the Civil War, which allowed the former slaveholders to regain political power. This action had the effect of denying to blacks the legal protections they were entitled to under the provisions of the Fourteenth Amendment. As citizens, they should have had governmental protection of their inalienable rights to life, liberty, and estate. It is clear that, at least in some Southern states, their political power had been usurped and, as a result, blacks were often tyrannized.[36] It is also clear that in many Southern states the governmental officials used race and racism as a basis for laws that restricted the political power of black citizens. One might think that all of this shows that blacks were not protected. But remember, Natanson's position is that being unprotected means that some blacks are not in a position to give consent. It is at this point that Locke's position on usurpation and dissolution of government becomes crucial to the discussion.

Locke and Black Americans

Locke's work is not totally applicable to the situation of blacks, particularly because Locke was concerned with individual and not group consent. I do think that his work has historical significance, however, because of the role his view played in the debate about what it meant to be a citizen of the United States. In this vein, Locke's position can give some insight into the problems of political obligation, civil disobedience, and the status of some black Americans, particularly since blacks were claiming that they were being treated unjustly and saw civil disobedience as a way to address social and political concerns.

Locke does have something to say about the misuse and abuse of political power by the government over citizens and their response to it. In chapters 17–19 of *The Second Treatise on Government,* Locke discusses usurpation of political power, tyranny, and the dissolution of the social contract. He discusses at length the relationship between usurpation and tyranny, concluding that:

As usurpation is the exercise of power which another has a right to, so tyranny is the exercise of power beyond right, which nobody can have a right to. And this is making use of the power anyone has in his hands, not for the good of those who are under it, but for his own private separate advantage—when the governor, however entitled, makes not the law, but his will, the rule and his commands and actions are not directed to the preservation of the properties of his people, but the satisfaction of his own ambition, revenge, covetousness, or any other irregular passion.[37]

Laws enacted under the guise of racism would be an example of irregular passion.[38] For some blacks usurpation came in the form of denying their legal and political rights, which caused these blacks, who were legally citizens and entitled to protection and the exercise of their rights, to have no say in the political arena. The political power of blacks had been usurped. Because it would be futile to attempt to cite all of the ways in which race and racism were used to deny blacks access to the political arena, for the purpose of this chapter, we can restrict our attention to the plight of blacks with respect to their participation in the political process.

With emancipation, two amendments, the Fourteenth and Fifteenth, were written into the Constitution especially to protect the voting rights of the newly freed slaves. These amendments specifically directed states to guarantee voting rights to black citizens.

Three civil rights acts were enacted between 1866 and 1875 as a way of assuring equality of treatment (including the right to vote) to America's blacks. These acts—the Civil Rights Act of 1866, the Civil Rights Act of 1870, and the Civil Rights Act of 1875—along with the constitutional guarantee, permitted black people in the South to exercise the right to vote with relative ease during Reconstruction. After Reconstruction, however, several states adopted so-called grandfather clauses, which restricted registration and voting to persons who had voted prior to emancipation. This practice was finally declared unconstitutional by the Supreme Court in 1915. With this defeat Southerners adopted the "white primary," through which the Democratic party prohibited blacks from participating in primary elections in nine states. When the white primary was outlawed, many Southern states resorted to gerrymandering as a way of disenfranchising blacks. In a long series of cases, the Supreme Court eventually curbed these practices, but blacks still lacked full participation in the political process.

The usurpation of political power was tyrannical in the sense that blacks were subject to laws they could not participate in making and, as free citizens, would not have given their consent to.[39] These blacks were denied both access to political information and the right to exercise their political rights. Many of the laws enacted without input from these blacks served to lower substantially the overall quality of their social and economic lives.[40] What did this tyrannical use of power do to the political status of blacks? Did this usurpation of political power force blacks back into a state of nature?

Locke makes a distinction between the dissolution of government and the dissolution of society.[41] The usurpation of political power by Southern governments did not dissolve society. Those governments were actually breaking the political trust by their actions. Blacks could have accepted the dictates of these governments and thus legitimated the usurped political power. But they did not, and, as Locke notes: "Unless the citizens freely consent to the governmental actions by accepting the new rules, this government is then at war with these citizens."[42] Blacks were still citizens and as such had the right to resist the dictates of the usurpers.[43] Those governmental officials who used the power they usurped in a tyrannical manner acted contrary to a trust.[44] The society, however, had not dissolved, and thus blacks were still full members of the state. Certain governmental officials had put themselves at war with those blacks. Politically unprotected blacks were in a position to morally resist the dictates of that government. They did not, as Natanson claims, remain in a "state of nature." These blacks were United States citizens under the provisions of the Constitution.[45]

If we take seriously the notion that states can decide who is and who is not a citizen and if persons so described act as citizens—for example, pay taxes, defend the state, and demand that the state protect their political rights as citizens, then they are citizens. At the passage of the Fourteenth Amendment, blacks became citizens and their children and their children's children would be citizens. If we want to talk in Lockean terms, these citizens should have been protected.

For many blacks, both the federal and state governments failed to ensure blacks equal protection as prescribed by law. Locke thinks that when this happens the goal of citizens is to get the legislature to act according to the trust for which it was established: to protect property, broadly defined.[46] It is important to remember that for Locke, citizens have the right to judge whether or not the governmental trust has been broken. Unprotected black citizens are to be the judge of what actions to take against the government, but, of course, they should try to act within the established political framework to have their concerns addressed. Locke seems to think that representatives will be responsive and address the civil wrongs, once they are aware of them. But if the government is not responsive, civil disobedience can then be seen as a legitimate method both to make one's plight a matter of public concern and to force the government to uphold its part of the social contract.[47] The results of the civil rights movement seem to support Locke's contention.

At this point, the following claims can be made: first, many blacks wanted to be citizens, and when they gained American citizenship, they showed that they were capable of carrying out the responsibilities of citizenship; second, the federal government did make an attempt to help in the adjustment from slavery to freedom; and third, Locke's position on usurpation and dissolution of government does not support the position that blacks were in a state of nature.

Black Americans and the State of Nature

How do these points affect the claim that present-day blacks are still in a state of nature? Obviously, they cannot still be in such a state if, as my reading of Locke and an examination of black political history show, they were not in it to begin with.

Does it matter, as Natanson claims, that some blacks have never been in a position to exercise their political rights and have never enjoyed the protection of the government? There is no logical inconsistency between not being protected by the government in the American-traditional model and being a citizen. It is possible for citizens to have rights on the books but not be protected against the violation or infringement of these rights by others, even in a liberal democratic state. A political life in a liberal democratic state is compatible with the existence of laws that are not enforced. It does not follow that these politically unprotected individuals are not citizens. It does follow, however, that those citizens who are politically unprotected are justified in protesting the lack of protection of their rights, in the American-traditional model.[48]

Consent, Citizenship, and Legal Standing

In the end, if we accept Natanson's position that some blacks are still in a state of nature, we encounter two more difficulties: first, if these individuals are not citizens of the state, their behavior cannot be seen as civil disobedience, but rather as an act of war against the state. It is a war they will lose. They can only claim rights as aliens, not as citizens. They must depend on the good will of those who are citizens (or perhaps some outside state) to try to convince the state to protect them and do whatever is necessary to make their citizenship real. It is unclear what legal claims they have against the state, however, since they are not citizens.

Second, to claim that some blacks are not genuine citizens is to deny the two conventional ways of assigning citizenship at birth. Legal scholars, it has been noted:

are generally content to distinguish between right of birth place (jus soli) and right of descent (jus sanguinis) as the two major alternative principles that states use in assigning citizenship at birth. They describe how different states use one or the other of these principles (or a combination of both) and discuss the problems posed for international order when the laws of different states conflict. They simply assume that people will normally acquire citizenship through birth and that there is nothing problematic about this. (States may permit citizenship to be acquired at a later stage but the very term used for this, "naturalization," suggests that birthright citizenship is the norm.)[49]

In the United States, being born in the country or to parents who are citizens makes one a citizen with all of the corresponding rights and responsibilities. To claim that some blacks are still in a state of nature is to claim that even though blacks are born in the United States, they are still not citizens.[50] The claim that some blacks, who have never relinquished their birthright citizenship, are in fact not citizens runs counter to our understanding of how an individual becomes a citizen of the United States.[51]

If Brock, Obadele, and Nantanson are correct, what then is the status of those blacks who are not citizens? Aliens? Anyone who claims that blacks are not citizens of the United States has to explain why these blacks are not stateless beings—that is, citizens of no state.[52]

Consent, Protection, and Citizenship

Natanson's paper is important because he realizes that an argument like Brock's needs to be supported by a theory of what would count as legitimate consent. Since Natanson does allow for tacit consent, he has to show why consent theory in general is not undermined. We need to ask: if some present-day blacks have not consented, what counts as consent for present-day whites?

Natanson's use of Locke's theory of governmental protection to provide the other theoretical framework for understanding the legal status of some blacks[53] only pushes us back one step. Now we need a clear statement of Locke's theory of political protection. I have argued elsewhere that we can understand what it means to be unprotected within the Lockean state without returning to the state of nature.[54]

Natanson is correct that consent to political protection and the government's protection of members are important aspects of Locke's political theory, but his claim that some blacks are still in a state of nature is not supported by a careful reading of Locke. Locke seems only to claim that the state provides them with more benefits—protection, in this instance—than they would have in the state of nature.

Accepting minimal protection from the state does not entail that one is not entitled to greater protection from the state, owing to considerations of equality. Sometimes the claim "S accepts O" means that "S believes that S is entitled to no more than O." Sometimes, however, "S accepts O" means simply that S will start with O and go on from there. Natanson seems to have ignored the latter possibility.

Locke, and then later Rawls, realized that persons can be treated unjustly in a liberal democratic state, but neither thinks that these unjustly treated individuals lose their membership in the state nor their legal obligations.[55]

In the final analysis, Locke's position on consent is more complicated than Natanson has allowed. Natanson placed emphasis on the wrong passages in *The Second Treatise*. If Natanson had focused instead on chapters 17–19, he would have seen that Locke might support the use of civil disobedience, as employed by black Americans in the civil rights struggle.

It is tempting, in view of the racial oppression in America, to think that many blacks do not have political obligations to the state. The use of a Lockean argument is a double-edged sword: while the argument seems to show that blacks have no political obligations to the state, it also seems to show that the state has no political obligations to blacks.

But a careful reading of Locke's work and an insightful reading of black history support, as do our laws on citizenship, the conclusion that politically unprotected blacks in the United States are citizens and, as such, have legal obligations to the state. Just as important, the United States has obligations to blacks.

Five.
Moral Discourse and Slavery

BILL LAWSON

AFTER two hundred and fifty years of chattel slavery and a scant twenty years after the Emancipation Proclamation, Supreme Court Justice Joseph P. Bradley, arguing against the Civil Right Act of 1875, which guaranteed equality of access to public accommodations, made the following claim:

> it would be running the slavery argument into the ground to make it apply to every act of discrimination which a person may see fit to make as to guests he will entertain, or as to the people he will take into his coach or cab or car, or admit to his concert or theater, or deal with in other matters of intercourse or business.[1]

Justice Bradley then states:

> When a man has emerged from slavery and, by the aid of beneficent legislation, has shaken off the inseparable concomitants of that state, there must be some stage in the progress of his elevation when he takes the ranks of mere citizen and ceases to be the special favorite of the laws, when his rights as citizen, or a man, are to be protected in the ordinary modes by which other men's rights are protected.[2]

According to Justice Bradley, any discrimination blacks faced in 1883 could not be seen as a result of slavery: "Mere discrimination on account of race or color were not regarded as badges of slavery."[3] The United States government, according to Bradley, did not have the authority to prohibit private acts of discrimination; that was the role of individual states. He also did not feel that there was enough evidence to support the claim that a denial of public accommodation was comparable to a "badge of slavery." According to Bradley, the Civil Rights Act of 1875 was unconstitutional.

Bradley's comments show, at worst, a crass attitude toward equality for blacks or, at best, a failure to appreciate the impact of slavery on the lives of both blacks and whites. Bradley raises many perplexing questions about the relationship of the United States government to those persons formerly held in bondage. His remarks point out quite clearly how the language we use to frame a group's political and social status can have an impact on the public policy regarding that group. The vocabulary used to denote the legal status of blacks shifted from property and chattel during slavery to citizens and rights after emancipation.

The Language of Citizenship

Language is used to express thoughts, but it also shapes thoughts. Language as the later Wittgenstein noted, influences thought.[4] Language shapes the contours of our mental images of the world; thus, for example, feminist theorists have shown how language influences our conceptions of the place of women in the world.[5] Linguists are now aware that our language has a sexist bias. If our vocabulary tends to foster a morally unsatisfactory view of a group, then it is difficult to recognize the claims of that group or to marshal the support needed to address the social problems facing them.

The vocabulary of moral/political discourse is important for addressing social wrongs. If language embodies certain sexist or racist assumptions, these assumptions will influence our attitudes toward women and racial groups. Words do not merely refer to our reality, they help to define it. If we are concerned with righting social wrongs, we must examine the language that frames our public policy.

Our moral/political vocabulary is morally unsatisfactory and inadequate for characterizing the plight of present-day black Americans. This, in turn, has serious social and political ramifications. Our moral discourse does not capture the reality of the legacy of inequality that blacks have experienced due to slavery and its aftermath. There is no word in our moral/political vocabulary that captures this state of affairs, and I shall argue that such a word or phrase is needed if we are to develop a just social policy. The simple thesis that ideas determine reality will not be defended here. The focus instead will be on the importance of language for the formulation of our ideas about black Americans and public policies.

Justice Bradley felt that recently emancipated blacks should be viewed as "mere citizens." The use of the term "citizen" in 1883 to express the political and legal status of blacks denoted a shift in the government's obligation to help blacks overcome the legacy of the slavery experience. Programs and policies to alleviate the unequal status of blacks could only be justified, according to Bradley, by claiming that black rights, as citizens *qua* citizens, were being abridged. But even these rights claims had to be balanced against the rights of other citizens. The term "citizen," however, as Gerald MacCallum notes, does not carry any suggestion of a history of submission or subjugation.[6] That a person has the status of a citizen tells us nothing about the social or political history of the individual prior to the acquisition of that status. Individuals who become citizens of a given state may have a history of social and political oppression, but there is no suggestion of this conveyed by the term. The term "citizen" is thus not adequate to capture the social and political history of formerly enslaved groups.

Bradley's view about how recently freed blacks should be treated depends on the political/moral vocabulary of citizenship, by which was meant a person who is a full-fledged member of a given state, with all of the corresponding rights and privileges. This conception of citizenship is rooted in the democratic liberalism of the eighteenth and nineteenth centuries. It places supreme importance on respect for the individual as the primary social unit. Each individual is said to have an inherent self-worth that must be respected. In the American political and social context, this conception has come to mean that the individual stands apart from any group of which he or she is a member. In our liberal democratic society, ethnic or racial groups have no political significance; only individuals have standing in the democratic state.

It has been well documented that black Americans were victimized by slavery and that they were subjected to gross social and economic injustices after slavery. Indeed, one of the justifications for the Civil War was making social and political freedom a reality for all persons born in America.

After the Civil War, blacks were formally declared to be citizens. As citizens, they should have been accorded the same rights and protections as white citizens. When blacks are called citizens, it is assumed that their political and social status is equal to that of other members of the state. This view of the political and social status of blacks is mistaken, as a review of their history will show.

After slavery, newly freed blacks did not have the same educational or economic advantages as white members of society. Thus, while legal slavery ended, blacks still suffered from unjust discrimination because of their former slave status. In America, skin color was taken as a sign of belonging to the despised formerly enslaved group.

It should be remembered that one of the justifications for enslaving blacks was that they were "aliens." Many rationalizations were given for slavery, but the most pervasive was the view that blacks were naturally inferior. As historian Winthrop D. Jordan has shown: "In the years immediately before and after the 1800s, white Americans often revealed by their words and actions that they viewed Negroes as a permanently alien and unassimilable element of the population."[7]

According to Jordan, many whites saw blacks as alien beings, subhumans, or brutes. Blacks were not seen as equal to whites in any manner, and many whites thought that blacks would never be able to become their equals. Slavery created in the minds of many whites negative images of blacks. For example, Thomas Jefferson thought that blacks and whites would never be able to live in peace in America. If blacks were freed, he thought, it would lead to a destruction of one of the two races.[8]

The most conclusive and clear statement of this view in the later slavery period was embodied in the opinion of Chief Justice Taney in the Dred Scott case:

They [Negroes] had for more than a century before [the time of the Declaration of Independence and of the adoption of the Constitution] been regarded as beings of an inferior order, and altogether unfit to be associated with the white race, either in social or political relations; and so far inferior, that they had no rights which the white man was bound to respect; and the Negro might justly and lawfully be reduced to slavery for his benefit. He was bought and sold, and treated as an ordinary article of merchandise and traffic, whenever a profit could be made by it. This opinion was at that time fixed and universal in the civilized portion of the white race. It was regarded as an axiom in morals as well as in politics.[9]

The general belief that blacks were inferior did not change after emancipation, nor did the attitudes about incorporating blacks into the social fabric of society. It is unnecessary to cite all of the negative social and political experiences of blacks after emancipation. We should, however, note some of the ways in which race and racism were used to deny blacks access to the political arena.

The government failed to stop Southern politicians from passing laws that, in essence, denied blacks the right to vote. Several states adopted so-called grandfather clauses or poll taxes which further restricted their right to vote. White primaries and gerrymandering were also used to deny blacks access to the political arena.

Besides such techniques, property, educational, and "character" requirements were used to keep black citizens from voting. Perhaps the most effective means of disenfranchising blacks, however, were intimidation and violence.[10] These practices were effective in denying to blacks an extremely important right: the right to participate in the political process.

Thus, contrary to the official liberal ideology, the chances of all individuals gaining something as important as political participation were not equal. In America, being black played an important role in being refused jobs, access to public accommodations, and political protection. Being black also made it difficult for individuals to be treated equally by the majority of the electorate, by the law courts, and by those who dominated the economics of the nation.[11]

Here arises the problem for people with a moral consciousness, those who are concerned to ensure that the liberal model works: What can be done to bring the social and economic status of blacks in line with that of white citizens?

First we must recognize that there is a residual aftermath of enslavement. William Julius Wilson, in his important work *The Truly Disadvantaged,* writes: "centuries or even decades of racial subjugation can result in a system of racial inequality that may linger on for indefinite periods of time after racial barriers are eliminated."[12] The social and political history of blacks in America is deeply connected to racism and the slavery experience. It is clear that blacks suffered a grave social injustice during the period of American slavery, but the impact of American slavery on the lives of blacks did not end with the Emancipation Proclamation.

Lexical Gaps and Social Policy

Since our language does not incorporate into its vocabulary the impact of slavery on blacks, it lacks a morphological and semantic basis adequate to the framing of policies for implementing programs to bring about true citizenship for blacks. The term "black citizen" does not capture the true political/social reality of black life.

When a language lacks a word to describe an event or a thing, philosopher Adrienne Lehrer has proposed that the lack suggests that there exists a "lexical gap."[13] The term "lexical gap" is "multiply ambiguous and has been applied to all sorts of instances where a word is, in some way or another, missing."[14] The only kind of lexical gap a speaker is generally aware of is a functional gap—the lack of a convenient word to express what he wants to talk about.[15] An example of a functional gap can be seen with our use of terms to describe items that happen to be partly furniture and partly sculpture:[16]

English has no convenient word for such objects. Furniture implies something [perhaps] functional and sculpture suggests something decorative and nonfunctional. One could coin a compound, sculpture-furniture or furniture-sculpture, but the result is rather long and speakers prefer short locutions.[17]

Is it necessary that all functional gaps be filled? While it is true that our language may not have words that express a particular concept, often there is no need for such words. Consider a recent "60 Minutes" television program where Andy Rooney claimed that we needed a name for the white stringy fiber that hangs from a banana when it is peeled. There appears to be no need for such a word. The reason is that even though one may attend to the removal of such fibers when eating a banana, one does not often, if ever, tell someone else to remove them.

Likewise, the phrase "man with stones in mouth" has no single word to express the concept. While it may be convenient to have a single word to express "white stringy fiber from a banana," at the present time it would serve no pressing communicative purpose. If there came a time when the white stringy fiber from a banana or men with stones in mouth became an important part of the social structure, however, we would probably create a word and the functional gap would be closed.

The functional gap may indicate an evaluation placed on the concept. We have a special word for a dead human because of its importance to us, while we do not have one for the white stringy fiber from a banana because it lacks importance. It is, of course, true that certain occupations do have terms that have special meaning for those in that field. Many of these terms do not, however, become part of the popular discourse.

In social and political relations it often takes a while before a new word can be introduced to fill a conceptual gap. Consider the lack of a gender-neutral word to replace the pronoun "he." There is no word to express that concept because until recently, it was not considered important. But now it is recognized that the absence of such a word often leads to continued use of words reflecting sexist attitudes.

Drawing on Lehrer's analysis, I contend that our political language suffers from a functional lexical gap. (If there is a functional gap, it does not follow that there is a conceptual gap.) The issue for black Americans is that, while some persons have the concept of the legacy of black subjugation, there is no generally accepted word that denotes this condition. The lack of a concise descriptive word hampers the framing of appropriate social policy. The American slavery experience serves to illustrate very well how the lack of a word to articulate a group's social status makes it difficult even to take a census:

In 1860, Hundley published *Social Relations in Our Southern States,* which sorted the South's inhabitants into eight categories. Hundley constructed a descending pecking order that ran from gentlemen and cotton snobs through yeomen and poor white trash to the lowly slave. Nowhere did he find a place for the South's free Negroes. Hundley's omission suggests the anomalous position of free Negroes in the stratified, hierarchical society of the slave South. Negroes were supposed to be slaves. Free people were supposed to be white. People who were free and Negroes did not fit neatly into the idealization of Southern society, yet 250,000 of them un-questionably existed in the slave states in 1860.[18]

As we know, the census is an important tool for framing and imple-menting public policy. To many Southern whites, the concept of a free black in the social and political structure of the South was unthinka-ble. Southern political ideology had a conceptual gap. Thus Hundley had no word to designate free blacks. For Hundley, the term "free black" was an oxymoron, a contradiction in terms. The conceptual gap resulted in a functional gap.[19]

When the political or social status of a group cannot be articulated in the political vocabulary, it is impossible to frame appropriate social policy for them. A similar condition exists today. There is no word to help us frame or conceptualize adequate public policy to elevate the social conditions of blacks. Let me be clear here: I do not deny that some philosophers have appreciated the social and political history of blacks, but they have no word to express this situation.

When a group has an unequal social and political status and there is no word in the moral/political vocabulary that describes their status, political/social theorists who attempt to conceptualize the problems lack the vocabulary necessary to make this group's plight felt by other members of the state. The lack of a word for accurately describing the situation of blacks has influenced thinking on affirmative action, com-pensatory education, busing, and other programs designed to achieve social justice. With no guiding word for blacks' postslavery political and social status, policy makers and social scientists have described their current condition in one of two ways: either blacks are described as "second-class citizens" because they are denied the means to make their citizenship meaningful; or it is argued that the social and political problems of blacks are no different from those of other groups who have faced hardships but who are now making their way, if not their fortune. It is clear that blacks are not slaves, but it is also clear that their holdings and opportunities are not on a par with typical white Americans, including later immigrants.[20]

Language and Governmental Policy

It may be objected here that while I have shown that no precise word exists that connotes the particular history of blacks, it is still unclear that we need such a word. It will be argued that since we do have terms like "oppressed citizen" and "second-class citizen" to denote unequal status, we can express the fact that individuals are not full members of the state. While this is true, the phrase "oppressed citizen" tells us nothing about how the person came to be oppressed. The word "oppressed" is used so much that, without qualification, it connotes a group or person being harmed in some manner. It may be true that adding the word "oppressed" to "citizen" gives more emotive force to the claim that the action is wrong or harmful, but this emotive force does not give us historical information about the specifics of the harm.

What about the term "second-class citizen"? While it is true that "second-class citizen" denotes that one does not have the status of full citizenship, it does not carry the necessary historical significance needed to express the situation of many black Americans. Even convicts can be considered "second-class" citizens. Aliens can be considered "second-class" citizens. In the case of convicts, we might think that they are deserving of this status. However, blacks do not deserve fewer opportunities because of badges of inferiority due to their history. Any modifier placed before the term "citizen," e.g., "oppressed," "black," or "second-class," does not convey the actual history of blacks.

It may be objected, some whites and the government have not been totally insensitive to the plight of blacks. There have been governmental social programs that were meant to address the historical problems of blacks. The New Deal, the War on Poverty, and Reagan's trickledown policies were said to address the special problems of blacks, particularly poor blacks.[21] But, quite to the contrary, these programs were aimed at the majority of American citizens and did not specially or effectively address the aftermath of slavery on blacks.[22]

It is now recognized, in the work of William Julius Wilson, that there is a segment of the black population that still suffers from the effects of slavery—the "black underclass." Wilson notes that social policy framed around either equality of opportunity or preferential treatment has failed to eliminate the economic or social inequality faced by this group. These approaches fail because they advance middle-class blacks but do not drastically change the position of the truly disadvantaged.[23]

But let us consider for a moment Wilson's comments about those programs that were based on the principle of equality of individual opportunity. This principle, according to Wilson, is the bedrock of the old civil rights movement, which emphasized the rights of minority individuals. This was in line with the basic assumption of liberal democratic thought.

It was assumed that the government could best protect the rights of individual members of minority groups not by formally bestowing rewards and punishments based on race or ethnic categories, but by using antidiscrimination legislation to enhance individual choice in education, employment, voting, and public accommodations. This position took its lead from Supreme Court rulings which stated that the Fourteenth Amendment was not a black-specific amendment. Equal opportunity was to be applied to individual standing and not groups. The individual, therefore, was the "unit of attribution for equality considerations," and the ultimate goal was to reward each citizen based on his or her merits and accomplishments.[24] In short, equality of opportunity meant equality for each individual citizen.

According to Wilson, this approach did not address the substantive economic and educational disadvantages of many blacks. Wilson adds:

There are some blacks for whom it is enough to remove the artificial barriers of race. After that, their entry into the American mainstream is virtually automatic. There are others for whom hardly anything would change if, by some magical stroke, racism disappeared from America. Everyone knows this of course. And hardly anyone is willing to say it. And because we don't say it, we wind up confused about how to deal with the explosive problems confronting the American society, confused about what the problem really is.[25]

This is my point. It is difficult for us to frame policy for those blacks who suffer from the cumulative effects of racism because our language lacks a word to give their status a life in the public's mind. When blacks are thought of as mere citizens, there is a mental picture formed of their status and their ability to navigate the political and economic system.

As Wittgenstein argued, linguistic practices are intimately joined to "ways of life" defined by communal practices, beliefs, and attitudes. Wittgenstein's later philosophy emerged after he traced his early errors in doing philosophy to naïveté about how language influences thought. In reflecting on those errors, he remarked, "A picture held us captive.

And we could not get outside it, for it lay in our language and language seemed to repeat it inexorably." Earlier thinkers like Francis Bacon were also sensitive to this danger: "People believe that their reason governs words. But words turn and twist the understanding."[26]

Let me make it clear that I am not claiming that all we need to do is create a word and the problem of racial inequality will be solved. My point is that without a recognition of the power of labels, framing policy becomes even more difficult.

Wilson goes on to argue that any program to end black inequality must be part of a hidden agenda. The hidden agenda is to improve the life chances of groups such as the ghetto underclass by emphasizing programs in which the more advantaged groups of all races positively relate.[27] What we must do, if Wilson is correct, is to mask our intent to help truly disadvantaged blacks. I disagree.

Wilson is aware that the majority of Americans would not look with great favor on monies being spent on what they take to be undeserving blacks. But if we had a word to direct attention to the legacy of slavery, perhaps whites and blacks would begin to recognize that the problems blacks face have historical roots, and that blacks are not just trying to get something for nothing. In this regard, programs can be publicly acknowledged to be directed toward a group that finds itself in a socially disadvantageous position because of its social and political history. Furthermore, in the United States there is a tradition and practice of developing programs for groups who have been victimized, e.g., Japanese victims of internment, among others.

Consider the following description: a person who has fled or been ejected from his country of nationality or of habitual residence for reason of race, religion, nationality, political opinion, or warfare, as a victim of Nazi, fascist, or quisling regimes. The word used to signify this type of person is "refugee." The word "refugee" has descriptive and emotive force. When we hear the word we know what questions to ask or at least we have some idea about the circumstances that give rise to the designation. Refugees are often given comfort and aid and, in the United States, frequently provided with assistance in starting a new life. The word focuses our attention and understanding on the historical plight of those who are called "refugees."

In a like manner, an example of a group giving credence to their history can be seen in the Jewish expression "victim of the Holocaust."

This phrase carries information about the history of the person so designated and it elicits social understanding of the person's plight. There is no comparable word that has been established for descendants of slavery. As I have said, any modifier placed before the term "citizen," e.g., "oppressed," "black," or "underclass," does not convey the social history of blacks in America.

What about the phrase "victim of American chattel slavery"? This phrase may be used to refer to blacks, but at the present time it has no recognized meaning. In a perverse manner, Confederate white Southerners who lost families, land, and status in the Civil War might want to claim that they were "victims of American chattel slavery." It is not evident that the phrase clearly denotes blacks.

In the United States, alienating racism has had profound effects on the lives of all Americans. Blacks were subjected to discrimination that caused them to be seen as less-than-equal members of the state. Being seen as less than equal undermines the self-worth of many blacks. Poverty and social deprivation plus racial discrimination can be a continuous crushing burden which presses a stamp of inferiority on its victims. These individuals often have little hope that they will ever share in the American dream.

Language and Affirmative Action

Without a word, it is difficult for policy-makers to convince other members of society that the situation of blacks has historical roots. The affirmative action debate can be used to illustrate this point. One argument often given to justify affirmative action policy is the backward-looking argument. Bernard Boxill states the basic backward-looking argument in this way:

Black people have been and are being harmed by racist attitudes and practices. Those wronged deserve compensation. Therefore, black people deserve compensation. Preferential treatment for black people is an appropriate form of compensation for black people. Therefore black people deserve preferential treatment.[28]

Boxill argues that the backward-looking argument is subject to two main criticisms: first, the claims to compensation through preferential treatment of black beneficiaries are unfounded or vacuously satisfied; and second, that any claims by blacks are outweighed by other considerations.[29] It is the first criticism that will be our focus here: blacks' claims of compensation are unfounded or vacuously satisfied.

This criticism has two major thrusts. First, those blacks who are qualified are not damaged by discrimination, for if discrimination were that bad they would not be qualified at all. Since they are qualified, they are less deserving than those persons who have really been wronged by discrimination. Boxill, rightly, notes that it is a leap of logic to claim that, because a black person has been successful, there must have been no discrimination, or that even if there was discrimination, the individual has not been harmed by it.

Boxill and Robert Paul Wolff think that it is clear that there was severe discrimination against blacks and that this harmed blacks as a group. Both Boxill and Wolff argue at length that it is *as a group* that blacks have been harmed. Boxill argues that the psychological harm done to blacks can be documented, while Wolff contends that to take the term "social injustice" seriously is to admit that individual membership in a particular group is relevant to our conception of social wrongs.[30] How else can we explain compensation to groups that find themselves victims of social injustice?

Even if we believe that there is social injustice, why should we think that the injustice suffered by blacks merits special consideration? Lisa Newton argues that blacks have no special claim for compensation because other groups have also experienced discrimination. What about American Indians, Chicanos, Appalachian-Mountain whites, Puerto Ricans, Jews, Cajuns, and Orientals?[31] Blacks are often reminded that other groups came to America and made their way without any special help. Most whites assume that the country is made up entirely of minority-group persons, all of whom have risen, mostly by their own drive as individuals. Why not blacks?

The argument goes as follows: How can you compare slavery to what was done to the Native Americans or other groups? All of these groups have suffered and no attempt should be made to elevate slavery over the wrongs that other groups experienced. Since everyone has suffered some injustice, it would be wrong to give special status to the suffering of blacks. Slavery is just one wrong among many.

This also seems to be Michael Levin's position. Levin argues that the harm done to blacks is no greater than the harm done, for example, to someone who is murdered because he is Jewish. Racial discrimination, according to Levin, is just one harm of many that people can be subjected to. Levin writes that he would rather be discriminated against than murdered. He adds that the murderer violates his rights and "handicaps my children much more seriously than someone who keeps me out of medical school." If, according to Levin, we allow that blacks are owed compensation for racial discrimination, we must also compensate the children of persons who have been murder victims. According to Levin, "there is nothing special about acts of discrimination."[32]

What is interesting about this line of reasoning is that it focuses entirely on the harm done to individuals and not to group wrongs. Boxill and Wolff realize that the social history of blacks as a group is very important both to understanding their present condition and to justifying programs that address historic wrongs. What we must realize is that blacks are the victims of slavery and this has had negative consequences on the life chances of most blacks. As Wolff notes:

Social injustice is injustice imposed on a real social group because of its group characteristics. Such injustice strengthens the social definition of the group as a group and leads thereby very frequently to such destructive consequences as the internalization of negative self-images by members of the victim group. Insofar as the group identity is rooted in a common position in the social relationships of production and distribution, it will be powerfully reinforced by institutional arrangements that serve the interests of the dominant groups.[33]

American chattel slavery is a clear example of a social injustice. The slavery experience does give discrimination against blacks a different slant. Blacks were not enslaved because of their individual behavior.

This does not mean that other injustices are not wrongs. If we take into account the impact of slavery on blacks as a group, however, we should elevate the status of this wrong over others. Coming to appreciate the impact of slavery as a form of social injustice on the present social and economic standing of blacks as a group helps us to acknowledge this fact.

We have a legal and moral tradition of rectifying social wrongs, but our desire to right wrongs is based on our conception of the fact that a wrong has occurred. Someone or something must direct our attention to the wrong. The impact of slavery and segregation on the life-chances of present-day blacks is one such wrong that needs to be better understood. We are reluctant to see the present social plight of blacks as the result of American slavery, given our lack of understanding of their unique social history in the United States. Our moral and political vocabulary reflects this deficiency. Supporters of the backward-looking argument will always be hard pressed to convince others that the social history of blacks is relevant without the help of a word to denote this history.

The Language of Moral Discourse

Moral language helps us to properly conceptualize the status of a group. While philosophers may work on principles of soundness and validity, usually individuals are moved by the emotive force of language. This point is Humean in that Hume recognized that the appeal to sentiment is often a powerful force in convincing persons to act or to accept social policies. In order to give the proper weight to the black slavery legacy, we must employ language that gives that experience evaluative force.

Generally speaking, evaluative terms apply to lines of conduct. They interconnect to form a rich language system that allows us to indicate whether (and to what degree) actions are justified or unjustified. For example, those who hold that South Africa's system of apartheid is morally wrong also hold that there is moral justification for its abolition.[34]

A word for the American slavery experience will give credence to the position that policies implemented to improve the social and economic standing of blacks are justified, not only in the minds of policymakers, but also in the mind of the general public.

It should be noted that because we introduce a word to denote being the victim of slavery does not mean that blacks are blaming present-day whites for slavery. It only gives formal recognition to the fact that present-day blacks are in a socially disadvantaged position and that this condition has historical roots. The United States government has taken historical factors into account in its formation of policy for addressing problems faced by certain groups.

We can take note of the provisions of the law to give compensation to United States citizens of Japanese ancestry for the injustice of the evacuation, relocation, and internment during World War II. The act is to acknowledge the injustice of internment; to apologize for the behavior of the United States; to provide an education fund to inform the public about internment so as to prevent the recurrence of any similar event; and to make restitution to those individuals of Japanese ancestry who were interned. At this writing, East Germany has apologized for the treatment of Jews during World War II, even though East Germany did not exist as a state then, and even though few of its present citizens were participants in the war.

Language and Slavery

The legacy of slavery still haunts the American consciousness. While a word by itself will not undo four hundred years of history, it is a start. It must be introduced in no less a manner than public recognition of the wrong and the establishment of educational programs about the impact of slavery on all Americans.

When Justice Bradley cast the status of blacks as "citizens," he set the tone for understanding how programs and policy for blacks were to be viewed. His use of the term "citizen" cast the status of blacks in a positive light, but it also impeded any attempts to argue for policy based on their former slave status.

As I have argued, the language we use to frame a group's political and social status has an impact on public policy regarding that group. This maxim is understood by, for example, pro-life advocates. They have changed the words used to talk about a fetus from "potential person" to "unborn child." To call a fetus an unborn child is to recast its status in a socially important way. An unborn child is thought to be a member of the moral community in a manner that an unborn fetus never will be. The language creates a picture of an infant who has to be protected. Consider the statements, "she wanted to murder the fetus" and "she wanted to murder the unborn child." The latter evokes strong moral feelings.

The shift from the use of the term "unwed mother" to "single parent" is another example of how the language can influence our thinking on social issues. "Unwed mother" has been taken to connote a women who has fallen from grace, while "single parent" connotes a person (male or female) taking on the duties of parenthood alone. Our governmental policies are now geared to making the treatment of single parents equal to that of two-parent families. Finally, consider the shift in public perception when the language changed to refer to persons as "developmentally disabled" rather than as "mentally ill," "retarded," or "handicapped." These are examples of shifts in group labels, and these labels have political importance because they are used to influence both policymakers and public opinion. These labels are image-laden, appealing as much to the emotions as to the intellect. Although they provide basic categories of rational analysis, they may simultaneously evoke responses that are neither analytical nor rational. This broader evocative power, the power to reach both mind and heart, gives the labels a political importance.[35] A word to denote the American slavery experience would have the same effect.

It may be objected here that what one needs is a distinction between choosing a word for reasons of public relations and propaganda and for reasons of morally justifying public policy. When a group has a social history that is deeply connected to the racist propaganda about it, it is clear that to get other individuals in the state to see the members of the affected group as victims will require some propaganda. Just saying that blacks have this history will not be enough; other members of the state and policymakers will have to be convinced. The language that we use to frame our arguments will be very important. This language will also underpin our moral theory.[36] If a situation is morally objectionable and we want the general public to appreciate the situation, the language we use to bring this condition to their consciousness will have a public-relations aspect. The language will set the tone for justifying policies to address the situation as well.

The importance of this aspect of language can be seen in the impact words have played in our understanding the black experience. From the beginning, language had to be crafted to justify the treatment of blacks.[37] As noted above, blacks were described as aliens, subhumans, heathens, savages, or brutes.[38] Consider the fact that for insurance purposes, slavers who threw their human cargo overboard during the middle passage called blacks "cargo" or "chattel." Both of these terms set a tone for how blacks were to be viewed as members of American society.[39]

What this meant was that the states could make legal and social distinctions between the treatment of blacks and other citizens of the state.[40] It is from these conceptions of blacks that we get historians and other commentators defining slavery as a paternalistic system.[41] Evaluative language played a crucial role in this effort. (In chapter 2, it was shown why paternalistic arguments fail.)

Recall, I am not claiming that things would improve dramatically for blacks if only there were a word which reflected the social and political plight caused blacks by their special history. This would simplify things a bit too much. After all, one might object that the white problem in relation to blacks is not so much that there is no word for the historical experiences of blacks as it is that whites do not wish to acknowledge their role in the oppression of blacks. In keeping with this line of thought, it might be pointed out that the reason why America responds in morally appropriate ways to refugees and Holocaust victims is that we can help them and feel sorrow for them without feelings of guilt. We can tell ourselves that the Holocaust is a German problem.

All of this may seem to cast doubt on the value of having such a word. But it seems clear that our moral and political vocabulary shapes how we think about social policy. If our language does not adequately describe a group's plight, how is that plight to be brought to the consciousness of the policymakers? While we do not want to overestimate the value of a word for denoting the social history of blacks, we do not want to underestimate its value either.

The history of slavery is a moral indictment on America. No one wants to take the blame. But recognizing that there is this history does not mean that you have to take blame for it. The history can still be part of our calculations of the problems groups face in their striving for equal standing. Some whites might feel pressured by attempts to make the slavery experience part of our moral discourse. Indeed, many blacks would rather slavery not be discussed. As we have seen, slavery has had an important impact on the lives of all Americans. If we know this is true, then we need to have our language reflect this knowledge.

While there is no doubt that blacks are United States citizens, the language of citizenship gives the impression that blacks have the same social and economic chances as whites.[42] From the citizenship stance, it is thought that blacks are players in the political and power arenas in the same manner as whites.[43]

In sum, the lack of a word is an indication of a lack of interest Americans have in making the slavery experience a part of our moral deliberations. For experience shows—consider the case of computers and music—that whenever an event has had a major impact upon the lives of people, new vocabulary is introduced.

What is important is that there is no word in English that can be used to characterize the plight of the descendants of slaves in our society. What is wanted is something on a par with "refugee." And what one must realize is that the fact that there is no such word is indicative of the interests and attitudes of the speakers of the language. We have single words for the things that are important to us, that we are concerned with. Language serves to focus attention. I wish to focus attention on the fact that while blacks are United States citizens, they are, by and large, the descendants of slaves; hence a word is needed. If no single word is available, then a short phrase will serve, but only if its meaning can readily be grasped, only if it serves to convey the right sense. For example, we might use the phrase "descendants of chattel slavery."

Our English language is a rich one, as the philosopher John Austin noted decades ago, in its ability to describe actions, especially immoral ones. This important aspect of our language is often forgotten. We have terms like "discrimination," "exploitation," "abuse," and "genocide" to characterize, explain, and guide us around the wrongs that can be inflicted on other persons. But our current language is not exhaustive.[44] It is not yet rich enough to have a term that denotes the unique history of black Americans.

Six.
Forgiveness and Slavery

HOWARD McGARY

T HE AMERICAN slave experience provides us with the opportunity to examine the best and the worst of human behavior. As we have argued, the slave narratives have proven to be an excellent source for those who want to know more about slavery and its aftermath.

An often neglected issue in discussions of slavery is the attitudes of slaves and the recently emancipated toward their former oppressors. There are studies, of course, which examine the conflict between blacks and whites surrounding the freeing of slaves. But it is ludicrous to think that the end of slavery eliminated the enormous resentment that blacks felt toward slaveholders after years of brutalization and dehumanization.

In fact, it would be preposterous to think that any human beings subjected to centuries of brutality and subjugation would simply forget their past and go on with their lives. This would be doubly surprising because, as argued in chapter 1, the end of slavery did not bring about the end of black oppression.

Given that slaves were not "Sambos," it is understandable that slaves and ex-slaves would harbor resentment toward their former owners and a system that allowed them to be held as slaves. What is remarkable, however, is the lack of resentment expressed by slaves and ex-slaves in their own accounts of their slave experiences. Consider the remarks by William Grimes about his master:

It grieved me very much to be blamed when I was innocent, I knew I had been faithful to him, perfectly so. At this time I was quite serious, and used to pray to my God. I would not lie nor steal. . . . When I considered him accusing me of stealing, when I was so innocent, and had endeavored to make him satisfied by every means in my power, that I was so, but he still persisted in disbelieving, I then said to myself, if this thing is done in a green tree what must be done in a dry? I forgave my master in my own heart for all of this, and prayed to God to forgive him and turn his heart.[1]

Three explanations have been advanced to account for this phenomenon. One attempts to explain it by making metaphysical claims about the forgiving nature of black people. Another focuses on the deeply religious commitment of black people. A third account questions whether slave narratives accurately reflect the true feeling of slaves, former slaves, and their descendants. According to the third account, either white editors removed or toned downed hatred and resentment in the narratives they published, or the writers themselves masked their anger and resentment in order to get their work published.

No doubt all of the above explanations have some bearing on the forgiving attitudes we find in the writing of slaves and former slaves, but there is another explanation that may better explain the high degree of forgiveness exhibited. I shall argue that there is an explanation rooted in rational self-interest that better accounts for this apparent forgiving attitude. Before we develop this explanation, however, let us consider in some detail the second explanation.

According to the second explanation, the forgiving attitude of slaves is due to religion. The explanation usually goes something like this: Christianity, with its focus on the hereafter and mercy, was a religion that was well suited to rationalizing the predicament of slaves. In a brilliant work on slave religion, however, Albert J. Raboteau challenges the idea that Christianity made slaves docile and accepting of their condition. He notes that slaves were publicly expressing the contradiction between slavery and Christianity as early as 1774. He also felt that slaves knew enough about the orthodox theology of the times to condemn the hypocrisy of Christian slaveholders. Raboteau cites the classic case of Josiah Henson, a slave who refused the opportunity to escape at one point in his life out of devotion to his master. He claims that Henson was the exception and that even Henson lived to regret what he called his "unpardonable sin." Raboteau doubts that the religion of slaves led them to place little regard on their worldly self-interest in favor of faith in the afterlife. His work can be used to question the belief that slaves displayed a surprising lack of resentment because of their religious convictions.[2] Raboteau's arguments are compelling, but I stop short of concluding that religion played no role in the apparent forgiving attitude that we find in a number of narratives. Before we explore the explanation that I claim is rooted in rational self-interest, however, we must have a better understanding of what we mean by forgiveness.

If forgiveness is compatible with self-respect, then it is hard to understand how normal human beings could be forgiving given the brutalities of slavery. If, however, forgiveness involves acting in ways that promote one's rational self-interest, then we may be more inclined to understand the apparent forgiving attitude of black slaves. If we can show that there were good self-interested reasons for blacks to forgive their oppressors, then we may have good reason to think that this fourth type of explanation is viable.

There are a variety of contexts in which the term forgiveness is used.[3] In secular contexts, we forgive breaches of etiquette, mistakes, and accidents. With some accidents and mistakes there is nothing to forgive, but when they are due to carelessness or recklessness we believe that forgiveness is an appropriate response. In sacred contexts we recognize divine forgiveness: God's forgiveness for our sins.[4] These are all interesting uses of the concept, but they shall not occupy us here. My concern shall be with forgiveness for acts of intentional wrongdoing involving mortals in secular contexts where the person wronged genuinely believes that he or she has been the victim of wrongdoing. This is the case with chattel slavery in the United States.

Forgiveness in these contexts is seen as a virtue, and virtues are always thought to be praiseworthy motives for action, even where the action that results is not itself thought to be praiseworthy. Virtuous acts and motives are things that we want to encourage because we strive to be virtuous persons. So, if forgiveness is a virtue, it would be useful to have a clear idea of the nature of this type of virtue and how it reflects on our moral characters.

Is forgiveness a moral virtue? I am inclined to think that it is. Many have thought that an important aspect of forgiveness is the role that it plays in keeping our resentment toward wrongdoing from going beyond appropriate limits. It is believed that if rightful resentment goes unchecked for too long, it will be so consuming that the resenting person will not be able properly to recognize and assess moral reasons.[5]

Forgiveness, then, might best be described as a virtue that allows us to keep our resentment within appropriate limits. (Of course, other virtues like kindness and generosity, when attached to acts of forgiveness, may be said to give such acts even greater moral worth.) We sometimes are able to get rid of our resentment without forgiving, however, because we have simply forgotten what caused our resentment.

Even the victims of serious wrongdoing are encouraged, after a time, to forgive and forget. This is thought by some to be necessary if the victims are to put the wrongs behind them and to get on with their lives. Perhaps if we have a better understanding of forgiveness, then we may be in a more advantageous position to evaluate such a recommendation.

We will, we hope, only infrequently find that we have committed acts that violate our sense of morality. But if we conclude that our actions were morally unjustified, we will feel a range of emotions: guilt, remorse, or regret. In fact, if one or all of these emotions are not present in an agent, we either doubt that the agent has understood the nature of the act or we conclude that the agent has a faulty character. These emotions tell us a great deal about our moral characters.

Because the feelings associated with emotions like remorse and regret are not pleasant, they serve to discourage us from engaging in actions that produce them. This is not to deny that our thoughts influence our judgments about what to do, but my point is simple: our emotions can help to shape our thoughts about what is morally appropriate or help us to do what is right.

Emotions like guilt, remorse, and regret and their relation to moral character have generated thoughtful discussions, but little attention has been paid to the role that forgiveness plays in the deliberations of a moral agent who has been the victim of some wrongful act. Perhaps this is because many writers have not considered forgiveness to be an emotion. Unlike regret or guilt, forgiveness, on their accounts, is not an emotion or feeling that we undergo, but something that we deliberately do under very specified conditions. For them, feelings are not essential for forgiveness. However, to say that forgiveness involves our feelings in an essential way is not to suggest that when we feel we are passive.

A major claim of this chapter is that the reasons for forgiving or failing to forgive can be self-pertaining and that forgiving or refusing to forgive primarily involves the forgiver's feelings about the elimination of resentment. I shall define later what I mean by a self-pertaining reason and, along the way, I shall make some points about the differences between forgiveness and other closely related virtues.

Forgiveness and Resentment

"Forgiveness" has been defined by Jeffrie Murphy as a cessation of resentment for moral reasons, where the cause of the resentment is wrongdoing or a breach of trust in some special relationship like a friendship.[6] It is important to note that we can resent a person and thus forgive them by ceasing to resent them for things that do not involve the violation of rights.[7] We can resent and forgive friends and lovers for failing to live up to expectations, even if it would be correct to say that we do not have a right to expect that they live up to these expectations. For example, we can forgive a close friend for failing to remember a birthday. Here I call your attention to the fact that we are often hurt or injured by actions that do not violate our rights. If we focus only on rights violations as giving rise to warranted resentment, then we omit an important class of acts where forgiveness might be an appropriate response.

By broadening the class of actions that may give rise to warranted resentment, we have set the stage for arguing that forgiveness is the correct response to a wider range of cases than we might have imagined had we restricted our focus to rights violations. This clarification is useful, but we are still faced with specifying what we mean by claiming that forgiveness is the "correct response." Do we mean that certain conditions require forgiveness as a matter of moral obligation, or do we simply mean that these conditions make forgiveness praiseworthy?

Most accounts of forgiveness require the intentional cessation of resentment as a necessary condition for forgiveness. There are very specific ways, however, that the resentment must cease to exist in order to satisfy this necessary condition. It will not do, for example, for the resentment to cease to exist because the passage of time has caused it to fade from the person's memory. Ceasing to resent because one has forgotten a wrong is not the same as forgiving. We should also be aware that a person whose warranted resentment is eliminated through hypnosis cannot be said to have forgiven. In order to satisfy this condition of forgiveness, the forgiver must intentionally cease to resent the source or cause of the sense of having been wronged.

To be sure, one might think that we should not be expected to give up all our resentment toward wrongdoing in order to be said to have forgiven a wrongdoer or a wrongful act. Would it not be morally permissible and wise to retain some of our resentment as a way of keeping ourselves on guard when it comes to future dealings with the person who wronged us? We would be wise to be cautious in our future dealings with such a person, but I do not think we need to harbor feelings of resentment in order to practice caution. We can do so by bringing to mind our thoughts about how we felt when we were wronged.

Returning now to the issue of forgiveness and the intentional cessation of resentment, Murphy has written: "my ceasing to resent you will not constitute forgiveness unless it is done for a moral reason. Forgiveness is not the overcoming of resentment simpliciter; it is rather this: to forego resentment on moral grounds."[8] Is it correct to say that when we forgive we always intend to do so? Can we not just realize that we have forgiven someone without having decided to do so? Murphy thinks not, and I agree. We sometimes do say that A has forgiven B for some wrong because A is a forgiving person. Does being characteristically a forgiving person allow us sometimes to forgive without deciding to do so? I think not. We do decide, but our decision may not require much deliberation because our forgiving nature makes us feel good.

Murphy's remarks are instructive, but he is not clear about what constitutes a moral reason. It appears that he has in mind moral reasons that relate to the offender, such as kindness to others or concern for the pain of others. I do not believe, however, that he truly appreciates that we can have moral reasons that relate to ourselves. Even if we accept that a moral point of view is not solely one of self-interest, a self-pertaining reason can still count as a moral reason for acting. By self-pertaining, I mean a reason that shows concern for the self without being selfish. The following quote from Murphy may help to support my interpretation of the way he unpacks moral reasons:

You have wronged me and I resent you deeply for it. . . . In short, my resentment so dominates my mental life that I am being made miserable. In order to gain my peace of mind, I go to a behavior-modification therapist to have my resentment extinguished. (Let us suppose there are such techniques.) Have I forgiven you? Surely not—at least not in the sense where forgiveness is supposed to be a moral virtue. For my motivation here was not moral at all; it was *purely selfish,* i.e. the desire to promote my own mental health.[9] (emphasis added)

Murphy is certainly right that removing the resentment through behavior modification with no regard for others casts doubt on whether the change in attitude counts as the sort of forgiveness that can be seen as a moral virtue.

Unfortunately, his example is not the best as an illustration of a person acting from purely selfish motives. A person who is in the miserable shape that Murphy mentions will cause pain for those with whom he associates; maybe his desire to rid himself of this crippling resentment has self-interest as an ingredient, but there can also be a component of "concern for the welfare of others."

The phrase "a concern for others" is ambiguous in this context. We could mean a concern for the offender—the person who caused the resentment—or we could mean a concern for persons other than oneself, but excluding the offender. Murphy seems to believe that in order to have a moral reason for forgiving, one must act for reasons that relate to a concern for the offender. I disagree. One may have such a motive, but such a motive need not be present for forgiveness to occur.

However, I think that Murphy is right that genuine cases of forgiveness cannot result from purely selfish motives, those that involve an indifference toward the welfare of others. The self-pertaining reason is motivated by considerations pertaining to the self, hence the propriety of the term self-pertaining; yet, because the reason has nothing whatsoever to do with a desire to maximize the satisfaction of one's desires at the expense of others, the reason is not properly called selfish. When we recognize this self-pertaining reason for forgiving, it can be seen that the exercising of a virtue can involve self-regarding but non-selfish reasons rather than being limited to other-regarding altruistic reasons. For example, Frederick Douglass's refusal to be beaten by the "nigger breaker" Covey can be thought to have exemplified the virtue of courage out of a desire to preserve his self-respect, a self-regarding reason rather than an other-regarding reason.[10]

Thus far I think we are safe in concluding that in order for X to forgive Y, X must intentionally cease to have some warranted resentment toward Y and X's reasons for no longer resenting Y should not be purely selfish (noting that a person can act out of a concern for self without being selfish). We have also unmasked the popular opinion that forgiveness necessarily involves forgetting the source of one's resentment. You cannot totally forget if you forgive. Forgiveness is incompatible with not knowing what it is that you are forgiving. If what I have said above is correct, X can cease to resent Y for some faulty behavior without X being required to forget that the faulty behavior occurred. In fact, for good prudential reasons, X may wish to keep the event in his or her memory in future dealings with Y, even though he or she no longer resents Y. Of course, if X constantly recalls Y's faulty action in order to put Y down or embarrass Y, then we may begin to wonder whether X has ceased to resent Y.

One might think that forgiveness does not always require the overcoming of one's resentment, because resentment is not always present when wrongdoing has occurred. Some wrongful acts may invoke pity in the victim rather than resentment. I doubt that this is so, however. In such cases, I would not deny that the victim could feel pity toward the wrongdoer, but I would still insist there is some resentment, even if it is not substantial.

Pardons, Compassion, and Forgiveness

Forgiveness is often closely associated with or tied to compassion and pardons.[11] However, forgiveness is conceptually distinct from these notions. When we pardon someone for the injury or wrongdoing that they have caused, we hold them responsible for the injury or wrongdoing, but for a variety of reasons we do not punish them even though they are responsible. For instance, we pardon or refuse to punish because we may think that greater harm would result to all by punishing rather than refraining from punishing the perpetrator.

When we pardon, the person who does the pardoning and the victim of the wrongdoing are not required to cease to resent the wrongdoer or his wrongful action. Overcoming resentment is not a necessary condition of pardoning. In fact, often the persons who most resent the wrongdoer are not the ones who are able to do the pardoning. Pardoning is a legalistic notion, and thus only certain persons within our web of linguistic and social conventions can complete the performative utterance of pardoning. Unlike forgiving, a person must occupy some official position or office in order to be able to pardon. It is also valuable to note that when we forgive, we do not condone. When we condone an injury or wrongdoing we are in a sense playing down the seriousness of the violation. In fact, if we were to minimize the seriousness of the violation that is forgiven, then we would detract from the forgiveness. As R. S. Downie has remarked: "the attitude of condonation is sometimes morally inappropriate, it cannot be the attitude of forgiveness, because the readiness to forgive is a virtue and the exercise of a virtue is never morally inappropriate."[12]

Is Downie correct that the readiness to forgive is always a virtue? Perhaps not. It is not clear that being too ready to forgive should be seen as virtuous. While listening to the evening news recently, I was somewhat shocked and dismayed to learn that shortly after the parents of a young woman who was brutally murdered learned the identity of their daughter's slayer, they said that they forgave the killer. If they really meant this, it would seem like a noble gesture. But to overcome one's resentment too quickly or not to resent at all when serious wrongs have occurred seems to me to be morally inappropriate. Perhaps religious duty requires us to do things like love our enemies and to cease to feel resentful toward everyone, even those who have seriously wronged us, but I do not believe that morality should make such stringent demands upon us.

Quite to the contrary, morality, for its maintenance, requires that we sometimes feel anger, resentment, and wrath, provided that they are kept within moral limits. If they are kept within their moral limits, they help us to recognize and avoid evil. The family who was so quick to forgive their daughter's murderer failed to appreciate that not being selfish hardly means being indifferent to what happens to one. When one forgives too quickly one reveals a kind of indifference to one's well-being. I admit that this example is somewhat complicated by the fact the person most directly wronged was the daughter, not the parents. Thus, some of what may be bothersome about the case is that we may think it is presumptuous for a person to forgive a wrong done to someone else when it only indirectly affects them, but I do not think that this complication invalidates my point.

The other virtue that is often closely associated with forgiveness is compassion. Compassion is an altruistic attitude, an emotion, and a virtue. As Blum remarks: "Characteristically, then, compassion requires the disposition to perform beneficent actions and to perform them because the agent has a certain sort of imaginative reconstruction of someone's condition and he has a concern for his good."[13] The phenomenon of forgiveness, on the other hand, does not require one to show compassion toward the object of one's forgiveness. The motive for forgiveness need not be a desire to relieve the suffering of the repentant wrongdoer. It could simply be to rid oneself of the destructive emotion of resentment that has gone beyond its appropriate limits. Remember, this motive is not purely selfish, because eliminating one's resentment by forgiving puts one in a better position to think clearly and respond appropriately in dealings with other people.

Forgiveness and Blame

When we say that someone is to blame, then we believe that they were in some way at fault for something considered to be wrong or inappropriate. In the western tradition, one must be accountable or responsible for faulty behavior in order to be held blameworthy. If this is right, then we cannot rightly resent someone for something that they were not responsible or accountable for. So it might appear that a necessary condition of X forgiving Y is that X ceases to blame Y for Y's faulty action. I think this is false. X need not cease to blame Y in order to intentionally cease to resent Y. There is a real sense in which we can still say that X no longer resents Y but still holds Y responsible for the faulty action. It seems perfectly sensible to maintain that I no longer resent you for killing my child, but that I still hold you culpable for the death of my child. You do not have to excuse a person for faulty behavior in order to forgive. Giving an excuse is a way of showing that their behavior was not blameworthy, or was less to blame than might have been thought.

I think we are now in a position to define more clearly what forgiveness amounts to by saying what it is not. It is not forgetting a wrong, although sometimes people who forgive do forget. We also have seen that it is not ceasing to hold someone culpable for wrong-doing, although, again, this may occur. It is also not the same as com-passion, but it can be motivated by compassion for others. Nor is it the case that when we forgive we thereby pardon. Thus far, the only clear necessary conditions for forgiveness are wrongdoing, or a breach of trust; intentionally ceasing to resent someone for their faulty behav-ior; and having reasons that are not purely selfish, recognizing that non-selfish reasons can still be self-pertaining.

Forgiveness and Action

Murphy has said: "Forgiveness is primarily a matter of how I feel about you (not how I treat you) and thus I may forgive you in my heart of hearts even after you are dead."[14] This claim has the ring of truth to it, but all, I dare say, are not convinced by it. Some would argue that I need not, in fact, cease to feel resentful toward you in order to forgive you, provided that I do not act in ways that would give a reasonable person cause to think that I harbor resentment toward you. Unfortu-nately, Murphy does not discuss this objection but chooses to explore instead reasons that moral agents may legitimately give themselves for ceasing to feel resentful toward someone who has wronged them.

Murphy points out that resentment is not always inappropriate. Sometimes it is an expression of our respect for the rights of others or our respect for morality. Murphy believes, however, following Bishop Butler's lead, that sometimes the feeling of resentment can dominate us and cause us to act unjustly due to passion. So, forgiveness is seen as a virtue "that functions to check resentment and keep it within proper bounds." According to Murphy, resentment oversteps its bounds when any of the following conditions obtain: (1) the wrongdoer has repented and has a change of heart; or (2) the wrongdoer meant well (his or her motives were good), or (3) the wrongdoer has suffered enough; or (4) the wrongdoer has undergone some specified ritual of humiliation (such as humbly begging for forgiveness); or (5) the wrongdoer has been a good and loyal friend in the past whose transgression should be seen as some anomalous occurrence.[15]

When one or more of these conditions is present, it serves as a moral reason for ceasing to resent. Murphy does not claim that these reasons are exhaustive, but each is sufficient to conclude that resentment has overstepped its bounds. We should be careful, however, and note that resentment can be out of bounds in at least two ways. It can be out of bounds at the start because it was exaggerated in the first place, or because it is allowed to linger for too long in spite of good reasons for ceasing to harbor resentment. Murphy focuses on the second problem, but the first issue is clearly relevant to any analysis of forgiveness that assigns a primary role to overcoming resentment. But if what I have argued above is sound, we can have additional self-pertaining reasons for not resenting too much initially and for overcoming our resentment and thus forgiving in time. Murphy resists the temptation to move to the religious realm, arguing: "there is moral insight waiting to be discovered if one will simply clear away some of the surrounding mythology."[16]

If we adopt the volitional theory of action, then we can define the nature of human action as follows: An agent has done something of type A, and his or her doing A is an action, just in case an event of type EA occurred as a result of the volition of the agent.[17]

On this account, forgiveness as an action must involve the agent doing something. There must be more than a mere speech act on the agent's part if we are to see him or her as acting in a forgiving way. For example, along with uttering the words "I forgive you," the agent may embrace Y, or act in generous ways toward Y, or undergo some personal sacrifice in order to help Y. If X acts in ways that provide others with good reasons to believe that X no longer resents Y, then X has forgiven Y even if X still feels resentful toward Y.

I do not think that, given such actions, X can be said to have forgiven Y. This is so even if in all of X's actions we can detect no element of resentment. I don't think that a person who acts in all the ways that would indicate forgiveness can be said to have done so unless he or she has undergone an emotional transformation and no longer feels resentful. Forgiveness serves to free the victim of wrongdoing of damaging resentment that has gone beyond its moral bounds, but it also can be used to set the wrongdoer's mind at ease when certain requirements have been satisfied, e.g., the wrongdoer has repented and has had a change of heart.

Supporters of forgiveness as an action or series of actions might respond that there is no need, from the moral point of view, to be concerned with a person's feelings if they do not somehow show up in actions. Since they believe that the primary purpose of morality is to insure that we do not inflict avoidable harm on others or violate their rights, from their perspective, as long as the victim of some wrongdoing recognizes and accepts that he or she has good reasons no longer to resent the person who has wronged him or her and acts accordingly, then there is no need for this person to undergo some transformation in feelings. Of course, they would add that such a transformation would be psychologically preferable but not morally required. In fact, they might add that it is likely that a person who did what he or she had good reasons for doing in spite of personal feelings might come to modify those feelings over time.

Advocates of this position also believe that by focusing on actions rather than feelings we put ourselves in a better position to identify a public criterion for determining if X has forgiven Y. We should distinguish, however, a public criterion for identifying an act of forgiveness from the conditions for forgiveness. Of course, what is meant in this argument is that the best means that we have for determining whether a person feels a certain way is by observing the way that person acts. The point is simple: another person's feelings are private; we don't have direct access to them. We can, however, have direct access to a person's actions. Unfortunately, this point made in support of forgiveness as an action confuses epistemology with metaphysics.

Some of the points made in support of forgiveness as an action are formidable, but there are also forceful reasons to recommend the position that forgiveness should be seen primarily as a feeling. Let us turn to an examination of those reasons.

Forgiveness as a Feeling or an Emotion

Emotions, like beliefs, have propositional content, but they also have a phenomenal character, i.e., when we have an emotion, we feel a certain way. In recent debates over the nature of the emotions there has been a tendency to define them as being more like beliefs than like feelings. Two reasons are frequently given to support this position: (1) feelings are not susceptible to normative appraisals while emotions should be; and (2) feelings do not have intentional content and emotions do. I want to avoid becoming embroiled in the debate over the nature of the emotions. The important points for our purposes here are the claims that feelings cannot be appraised normatively and lack intentional content. My interest in these claims lies in how they relate to our discussion of whether forgiveness is an action or an emotion.

If we regard forgiveness primarily as a feeling, then we cannot give any normative appraisal of forgiveness and we cannot assign any intentional content to a feeling of forgiveness. Let me briefly explain these criticisms. We want to be able to make normative judgments about forgiving or failing to forgive. However, if forgiveness is a feeling, then some are inclined to say that feelings are incorrigible. The second objection is that feelings are not directed at objects or states of affairs. For example, tickles and pains lack intentional content although they may have an intentional focus.

But as Robert Kraut has clearly pointed out, the conclusion that all feelings lack intentional content is surely unwarranted. He demonstrates this from an examination of some feelings that do lack intentional content: "Even if feelings lack 'intrinsic' intentional content, they may nonetheless acquire such content by virtue of their position in a causal-counterfactual and normative network that ties them to environmental input, to action, and to one another."[18] So it is still an open question whether some feelings have intentional content. We do not have to have certain thoughts in order to feel tickled, but forgiveness may be one of the feelings that does have intentional content.

Kraut argues persuasively against the objection that emotions should not be understood as feelings because this would rob them of their quality of being susceptible to normative appraisal. He shows that emotions are social constructions. In other words, they are not mere cognitions. Emotions, on his account, do not involve judgments or evaluations as necessary constituents. They gain this attribute from the environment or social context. Thus, they are still subject to normative appraisals because they are subject to an institutional and contextual dependency. This dependency allows us to evaluate the emotions.

Kraut's contribution to the discussion of emotions is important. He gives us a well-worked-out account of the psychological theory that an emotion is a feeling in a certain context. For Kraut, an emotion should not be understood as the exclusive domain of discrete individuals, but rather as experienced, identified, and made legitimate by their social context. Thus, understanding emotions is a contextual exercise, and feelings are understood to have a much richer sense than philosophers and cognitive psychologists have been willing to admit. If Kraut is correct, then we are still able to sensibly utter things like: X should feel forgiving toward Y. On this account, it does make sense for people to have access to or criticize their feelings. We do not have to view all feelings as bodily sensations like tickles, and we do not have to make something a belief before it can be placed in a normative context.

It is my contention that when we succeed in forgiving another it involves positively transforming our feelings toward the offender. I do not deny that we primarily concentrate on the actions of the forgiver when we look for evidence of forgiveness, but evidence for the occurrence of a phenomenon is not identical to the defining features of it. We should not confuse epistemology with metaphysics.

As anyone who has struggled to forgive an offender is well aware, it is typically not an easy thing to do. I believe that we can attribute the difficulty associated with forgiving, in part, to the fact that we must undergo an emotional transformation, and this is sometimes very difficult to do. Although our emotions involve thoughts, they are not identical to our thoughts. Sometimes having an emotion involves having an object in thought as the focus of our emotion, but sometimes there is no such object in focus.

Even in cases where an offender has provided us with rational grounds for recognizing that he or she has transcended a wrongful act, we still may be unable to divorce the offender from the offending acts. Sometimes our emotions provide us with tendencies to act on the grounds that we have recognized something to be desirable or undesirable, but it is not at all clear that emotions *necessarily* involve such tendencies to act, even when we make a positive appraisal of the potential for action. We still may be unable to put ourselves in a certain emotional state even though we desire to do so.

After our discussion of forgiveness as an emotion, I think we can identify our final necessary condition for forgiveness to occur: that the person doing the forgiving undergo an emotional transformation. The person must cease feeling resentful toward the offender in spite of the offender's wrongful action.

Is There a Duty to Forgive?

When a person is said to have a duty or an obligation to do something, then that person is required to do that thing. Are we morally required to forgiven each other? In the Christian tradition, forgiveness between mortals is seen as a gift or an act of love, a mark of the religious person. From the perspective of the forgiving person, forgiveness is seen as a means of demonstrating Christian love by doing something positive both for others and for oneself (by ridding one's heart and soul of negative feelings toward fellow human beings, especially the feelings of resentment).

On the other hand, in Jewish thought forgiveness is viewed as an obligation.[19] In fact, in this tradition, even when a person mistakenly believes that he or she has wronged another and thus takes the proper steps to give the presumed victim moral reasons for forgiving him, that forgiveness is an obligation, even when the alleged victim is certain that he or she has not been wronged.[20] Of course, the alleged victim should attempt to convince the mistaken transgressor that he or she has not acted wrongly, but in the end, if the attempt does not succeed, then he or she is required to forgive the mistaken transgressor. So, on this account of forgiveness, overcoming resentment is not a necessary condition. (It could not be, in cases like the one I just described.)

I cannot accept the idea that we can forgive without overcoming resentment. Nor can I accept the view that we are required to forgive persons who have not wronged us. Of course, we can pretend for moral reasons to forgive someone who persists in mistakenly believing that he or she has acted wrongly toward us; this, however, is only a pretense. It is not a genuine case of forgiveness. But what about cases where a person has wronged another and provides good moral reasons for forgiveness of the sort that Murphy describes? Are we under a moral obligation to forgive such persons?

One might believe that forgiveness is required in certain circumstances because morality will not allow us to turn a deaf ear to the suffering of another human being if we have the wherewithal to limit that suffering without destroying or causing serious harm to ourselves. The problem with this belief is this: if we make forgiveness a moral duty, then we must see it as a substantive virtue. I want to resist this move because I think we have good reasons for seeing forgiveness as more like the virtue of courage than like honesty. We strongly hope and expect people to be honest, but we do not expect people to be courageous. In fact, we will disassociate ourselves from people who are known to be dishonest, but we do not think it necessary to cease dealing with someone because they are not courageous. Of course, soldiers in time of war may come to expect their comrades to be courageous, but this is because of the special acknowledged relationship of dependency that exists between soldiers in combat situations.

It is clear that courage and honesty are praiseworthy motives, even if good consequences do not always result from them. What is not clear, though, is whether we have a moral duty to feel or act in ways required by these different types of virtue. Kant certainly believed that we have a moral duty to be honest.

The debate between Kantians and consequentialists over the supposed right to tell lies from benevolent motives need not detain us here. My point is simply that a better case can be made for honesty as a duty than for courage or forgiveness. In cases where a wrong is of a trivial sort, there is very little resentment and thus not much willpower is needed to overcome the inclination to continue to feel resentful. In the real test cases where persons have been the victims of gross wrongdoing, however, some effort is required to overcome the strong inclination to continue to feel resentful and perhaps to act in resentful ways. Do we want to say to the victims of these gross wrongs that they always have a duty to forgive if they are to maintain good moral standing? I think not.

Ironically, some Jewish writers on the Holocaust have rejected the idea of a duty to forgive when they urge Jews never to forgive the perpetrators of the Holocaust even if there are strong other-regarding reasons to do so. The same point has been made by black writers about slavery. Forgiveness, in their view, is supererogatory, not obligatory. Although we do want to promote and encourage the virtue of forgiveness in people, we do not want to do so by requiring them to forgive. Forgiveness must remain supererogatory if it is to serve its function of truly ridding us of our consuming resentment. Remember, resentment has, under appropriate conditions, a proper moral function. But we should also remember that we can have strong self-pertaining reasons for forgiving.

In the end, however, forgiveness should not be described as a gift given by the one transgressed upon to the transgressor for reasons ultimately to be decided by the one who has suffered the transgression. For if it is understood as a gift, there is the presumption that the giver is doing something to please the beneficiary. On my account, a person need not desire or hope to please the wrongdoer by forgiving him. Remember, we can forgive the dead. If what I have argued above is sound, then the reasons for forgiving or failing to forgive primarily involve the agent's feelings about the elimination of resentment.

I have only scratched the surface of this important topic. There are a number of issues that could stand to benefit from being subjected to philosophical scrutiny, e.g.: "Does forgiveness admit of degrees?" and "Can a morally good person be incapable of forgiving?" These and other interesting questions must await another occasion.

Slavery and Forgiveness

As the work by Bernard Boxill, Thomas Hill,[21] John Rawls,[22] and Laurence Thomas[23] shows us, self-respect is an important good. In fact, of the list of goods, it clearly carries a great deal of weight. Rawls, for example, has argued that no amount of material possessions can compensate for the loss of self-respect.[24] Thomas gives self-respect similar weight and goes on to claim that self-respect, unlike self-esteem, is not tied to a person's abilities and talents. For Thomas, self-respect focuses on a being's sense of his or her moral value rather than abilities. This does not mean, of course, that the person is morally good, but rather that the person believes that he or she is the type of being who has moral value. Boxill echoes this view: "a person can have self-respect and few other good qualities."[25]

Now, even if a person has a secure sense of his or her value, and thereby self-respect, this does not mean that it cannot be lost. Since self-respect is an important good, rational people do not want to lose it. In fact, numerous stories recount the lengths to which people from all walks of life are willing to go in order to preserve their self-respect.

But having and maintaining self-respect is not an easy thing to do even in the best of circumstances, so you can imagine how tough it must be for people who are in the grips of deprivation and oppression to maintain a good self-concept. Slavery was an institution characterized by brutality, deprivation, and oppression, so it stands to reason that slaves had to struggle to maintain their self-respect. Given this fact, the slave experience may prove to be useful in gaining a better understanding of what it meant for slaves to act virtuously and yet retain a sense of self-respect. We are particularly interested in what it meant for a slave to exemplify the virtue of forgiveness in a hostile environment that constantly assaulted his or her dignity and self-concept.

Above, I argued that forgiveness can be motivated by self-pertaining reasons. The inspiration for this view came from my reading of the literature on slavery, particularly slave narratives. The basic idea is that oppressed and powerless people may be motivated to forgive for reasons that might be quite different from those of free and powerful persons.

One thing that clearly comes across in the slave narratives is the constant assault on the dignity and self-respect of slaves. But what is also very apparent, as I have indicated, is the complex human and social relationships that existed between slaves and their oppressors. It would be too simplistic to say that slaves hated their oppressors and that was that; to do so would distort the varied forms of master-slave interaction.

These complex relationships give rise to an interesting set of questions. Was it harder for slaves to forgive when the moral climate systematically called their self-respect into question? Do those who endure profound systematic oppression have to be more cautious about forgiving a wrongdoer than the free and powerful, for fear that being prepared to forgive too easily is indicative of a lack of self-respect? Let us now turn to an examination of these related questions.

We can all readily agree that the person who easily and quickly forgives those who have committed serious wrongs against him or her accomplishes a feat that sets him or her apart from most persons. We can also agree that being inclined to forgive those who have wronged us is generally a good thing. But, as I have argued, whether a person in fact forgives another involves the assessment of reasons they have for forgiving (which can involve self-pertaining reasons), as well as overcoming certain potentially destructive emotions like resentment. As I have said, sometimes those who have strong reasons for forgiving are still unable to do so because they still harbor feelings like resentment. So, according to my account of forgiveness, forgiving is not as voluntaristic as it is often made out to be.

A real worry for oppressed and powerless people who are inclined to be forgiving in their nature is whether acting on their inclinations signals that they do not hold themselves in the proper regard. Slavery is an acute illustration of this worry because the institution called into question the humanity and moral standing of slaves. So, to quickly or easily forgive those who were a party to this dehumanizing way of treating and viewing people might tend to undermine their own convictions about their moral worth.

Boxill, commenting on the self-respect of the alleged servile slave or "Sambo," writes:

In sum, a person with self-respect may lose it. He may not be confident of always having it. He may not even be sure that he really has it. But if he does have self-respect, he will never be unconcerned about the question of his self-respect. Necessarily he will want to retain it. But no one will be satisfied that he has it. Hence the self-respecting person wants to know that he is self-respecting.[26]

Clearly what Boxill is saying is that we all need evidence for our claim that we have self-respect, especially those who are powerless and who are subjected to dehumanizing, oppressive practices. We need evidence because, as human beings, we are subject to exaggeration, distortion, and self-deception. This evidence will allow us to discount the claim that we are improperly assessing our self-respect. Speaking about self-respect and protest, Boxill argues that protest serves as good evidence for slaves who may be in doubt about their self-respect because they have been forced to feign servility in order to prevent serious harm to themselves or their loved ones.

What about those slaves and descendants of slaves who still suffer because of the racist actions of white oppressors? When slaves speculated about whether or not they should forgive their oppressors, what could count as appropriate evidence that their willingness to forgive does not count as a lack of self-respect? In order to provide an answer to this question, we must recognize that there were a host of actions, practices, and rules that comprised what we call the institution of slavery. So, when we talk about slaves forgiving, we must be clear about what they are forgiving. We could have in mind ex-slaves forgiving former slaveholders for holding them as slaves; slaves forgiving slaveholders and slavedrivers for acts of cruelty; or descendants of slaves forgiving those who engaged in wrongdoing against their ancestors.

Let us begin by examining the case where slaves forgive slavedrivers and slaveholders for acts of cruelty. This case is perhaps the most complex in regard to forgiveness and self-respect, because the slaves are called upon to forgive persons who continue to willingly participate in a system that denies them basic human rights. In such cases, it is hard to see how one could have proper regard for oneself as a full-fledged human being if one forgives those who continue to engage in practices that call into question one's human dignity. But as I said earlier, wrongdoing evokes a range of emotions in normal human beings, resentment being one of them. I also said the emotion of resentment, or an emotion similar to it, is the proper response as long as it is kept in check. For if the emotion is allowed to become dominate or linger for too long, it can have disastrous effects on the agent. So these are what I referred to earlier as self-pertaining reasons why a person would choose to let go of this feeling of resentment.

In typical cases of wrongdoing, letting go of the emotion presents no special problem because the wrong that triggered the emotion is over or behind one. In our first case of slavery described above, however, the wrongdoing continues to exist. Therefore, slaves in these circumstances are caught in a dilemma. They want to be able to get rid of their resentment because of the toll it takes on them, but to do so would be to ignore or underestimate the nature of the injustice they are being forced to endure. There is a conflict between holding on to their self-respect as persons who do not condone or capitulate to injustice and, at the same time, letting go of the rightful resentment they feel because of this injustice.

This is a serious conflict that must be resolved in the healthy personality. Unfortunately, this dilemma turns out to be an additional wrong of slavery that continues to plague present-day African-Americans. The dilemma, for emancipated slaves, African-Americans during the Jim Crow era, and present-day African-Americans is not equally stark. Nevertheless, it still exists. It is no surprise that self-respect is a crucial theme in the writings of contemporary African-Americans.[27] As the wrongs of slavery and unjust discrimination lessen, then so does the emotional conflict that results from a natural response to injustice. Until these wrongs can be said to be behind African-Americans, however, it is extremely difficult for them to adopt a forgiving posture even though there may be self-pertaining reasons for doing so. So, if what I have argued above is sound, forgiveness is a virtue that is extremely difficult to exemplify by people who have been subjected to prolonged and systematic oppression that calls into question their very status as full-fledged persons. But what is quite surprising is that African-Americans have been able to grab the dilemma by the horns and progress in spite of it.

Hatred, Revenge, Retribution, Vengeance, and Forgiveness

I have argued above that forgiveness, when properly understood, is a way for ex-slaves to get rid of a resentment that, over time, could become consuming and counter-productive. There might, however, be other morally acceptable ways that this crippling resentment can be overcome.

One possible way that comes to mind is what Jeffrie Murphy and Jean Hampton have called righteous hatred: hatred that does not flow from spite, but that is retributive in nature. By retributive, they mean hatred that has as its object restoring the proper moral balance that has been upset by wrongdoing. Unlike spiteful hatred, those who feel righteous hatred are willing to openly and publicly avow their feelings.[28] Murphy and Hampton argue that there is a place for righteous hatred provided that the emotion or attitude is seen as dangerous and prone to blind passion.

Even righteous hatred, however, cannot play the role that I have assigned to forgiveness. For righteous hatred, like resentment, is an emotional response that can and often does get out of hand, because the wrongs that cause righteous hatred are always of a grievous sort. For this reason, I doubt that righteous hatred can help one to keep one's emotional and moral state in the proper balance. Substituting righteous hatred for resentment does not address the problem.

But perhaps righteous hatred can lead to something that can allow persons to do away with their consuming resentment without forgiving. Maybe revenge, retribution, or vengeance can play this role. These acts might allow slaves and ex-slaves to get rid of their resentment and settle the moral score by punishing the wrongdoer.

These responses could work in the proper context: where the slaves had the power to revenge their wrongs, take vengeance, and demand retribution. But these responses were highly unrealistic for the overwhelming majority of slaves and ex-slaves. All of them require that the slaves through their own initiative demand or extract satisfaction from their oppressors. This was extremely difficult or next to impossible for slaves and ex-slaves to do without risk to life and limb. If they tried, failed, and lived, instead of easing their resentment they would more than likely intensify it. Therefore I doubt that revenge, retribution, or vengeance could substitute for forgiveness in the slavery situation.

Some may object that my account of forgiveness fails to capture an important aspect of it, namely love for others. It might be argued, in the spirit of Christianity, that forgiveness is a demonstration of the Christian proverb of "love thy neighbor." According to this interpretation, unconditional love for others is sufficient reason for forgiving even those persons who persist in transgressing against us. No doubt this interpretation may accurately describe the behavior of some slaves, ex-slaves, and their descendants, but I question whether it is a sufficient explanation in most cases. I do not deny that many slaves embraced Christianity, but I do doubt that their commitment to Christianity is the only viable explanation for why slaves were able to exemplify the virtue of forgiveness under the most adverse of circumstances.[29]

NOTES

Philosophy and American Slavery

1. See, e.g., William J. Anderson, *Life and Narrative of William J. Anderson: or, Dark Deeds of American Slavery Revealed, Written by Himself* (Chicago: Daily Tribune Book and Job Printing Office, 1854); Charles Ball, *Slavery in the United States: A Narrative of the Life of Charles Ball, a Black Man, Who Lived Forty Years in Maryland, South Carolina, and Georgia as a Slave* (New York: John S. Taylor, 1837); Henry Bibb, *Narrative of the Life of Henry Bibb, an American Slave, Written by Himself* (New York: By the author, 1850); Linda Brent, *Incidents in the Life of a Slave Girl* (Boston: By the author, 1861); Isaac Brown, *Case of the Slave Isaac Brown: An Outrage Exposed!* (n.p.: n.p., 1847); Jane Brown, *Narrative of the Life of Jane Brown and Her Two Children: Related to the Reverend G. W. Offley* (Hartford: Published for G. W. Offley, 1860); William Wells Brown, *Narrative of William Wells Brown, a Fugitive Slave, Written by Himself* (Boston: Anti-Slavery Office, 1847); Annie L. Burton, *Memories of Childhood's Slavery Days* (Boston: Ross Publishing Company, 1919); William Craft, *Running a Thousand Miles for Freedom: or, the Escape of William and Ellen Craft from Slavery* (London: W. Tweedie, 1860); Dinah, *The Story of Dinah, as Related to John Hawkins Simpson, after Her Escape from the Horrors of the Virginia Slave Trade, to London* (London: A. W. Bennett, 1863); Frederick Douglass, *Narrative Life of Frederick Douglass, an American Slave. Written by Himself* (Boston: Boston Anti-Slavery Office, 1845); Elleanor Eldridge, *Memoirs of Elleanor Eldridge* (Providence: B. T. Albro, 1847); Josiah Henson, *Truth Stranger Than Fiction: Father Henson's Story of His Own Life* (Boston: John P. Jewett, 1858); Elizabeth Keckley, *Behind the Scenes by Elizabeth Keckley, Formerly a Slave, but More Recently Modiste, and Friend to Mrs. Abraham Lincoln: or, Thirty Years a Slave, and Four Years in the White House* (New York: G. W. Carlton, 1868); Solomon Northup, *Twelve Years a Slave: Narrative of Solomon Northup, a Citizen of New York, Kidnapped in Washington City in 1841 and Rescued in January, 1853, from a Cotton Plantation Near Red River in Louisiana* (Buffalo: Derby, Orton and Mulligan, 1853); Ralph Roberts, "A Slave's Story," *Putnam's Monthly* 9 (June 1857), 614–20; and Sojourner Truth, *Narrative of Sojourner Truth, a Northern Slave, Emancipated from Bodily Servitude by the State of New York, in 1828* (Boston: By the author, 1853).

2. See, e.g., R. M. Hare, "What Is Wrong with Slavery?" *Philosophy and Public Affairs* 8: 2 (1979), 103–21, and John Rawls, *A Theory of Justice* (Cambridge, Mass.: Harvard University Press, 1971).

3. Ulrich Bonnell Phillips, *American Negro Slavery: A Survey of the Supply, Employment and Control of Negro Labor as Determined by the Plantation Regime*

(New York: D. Appleton and Company, 1918; rpt. Baton Rouge: Louisiana State University Press, 1969).

4. John W. Blassingame, *The Slave Community: Plantation Life in the Antebellum South* (New York: Oxford University Press, 1972).

5. For a discussion of the value of looking at what slaves had to say about their enslavement, see Charles T. Davis and Henry Louis Gates, Jr., eds., *The Slaves' Narrative* (New York: Oxford University Press, 1985).

6. For a discussion of the value of slave narratives, see Marion Wilson Starling, *The Slave Narrative: Its Place in American History* (Boston: G. K. Hall, 1981).

7. John Blassingame, "Using the Testimony of Ex-Slaves: Approaches and Problems," in Davis and Gates, *The Slaves' Narrative*, pp. 78–97.

8. John Blassingame, *Slave Testimony* (Baton Rouge: Louisiana State University Press, 1977), p. lxv.

9. Robert B. Stepto, "Distrust of the Reader in Afro-American Narratives," in Sacvan Bercovitch, ed., *Reconstructing American Literary History* (Cambridge, Mass.: Harvard University Press, 1986), pp. 300–22.

10. In Gilbert Osofsky, ed., *Puttin' On Ole Massa* (New York: Harper & Row, 1969), p. 10.

11. Ibid., p. 12.

12. Ibid., p. 11.

13. John Blassingame notes: "Because of this high proportion of exceptional slaves among the black autobiographers, their stories must be used with caution. It does not follow, however, that they should be dismissed as totally unrelated to the experiences of most slaves. Research based on this principle violates logic and accepted historical canons. Historians frequently draw their portraits of American character from the autobiographies of such exceptional whites as Benjamin Franklin, Mary Antin, Davy Crockett, Andrew Carniegie, Lincoln Steffens, John D. Rockefeller, and Henry Adams. Yet, some scholars reject the narratives because they were allegedly written by the most perceptive of former slaves. Historians cannot have it both ways. Logically, the comments of exceptional whites and exceptional blacks have the same strengths and weakness. An argument for or against using one applies equally to the other." Blassingame, *Slave Testimony*, pp. xli–xlii.

14. See, e.g., David Brion Davis, *The Problem of Slavery in Western Culture* (New York: Oxford University Press, 1966); Ann Lane, *The Debate over Slavery: Stanley Elkins and His Critics* (Urbana: University of Illinois Press, 1971); and James C. Morgan, *Slavery in the United States: Four Views* (Jefferson, N.C.: McFarland, 1985).

15. Sociologist Orlando Patterson attempts to show the impact of slavery on the psychological and sociological well-being of blacks. See Orlando Patterson, *Slavery and Social Death* (Cambridge, Mass.: Harvard University Press, 1982).

16. Stanley Elkins, *Slavery* (Chicago: University of Chicago Press, 1976), p. 82.

17. See, e.g., James D. Anderson, "Political and Scholarly Interests in the 'Negro Personality': A Review of *The Slave Community,*" in Al-Tony Gilmore, ed., *Revisiting Blassingame's "The Slave Community"* (Westport, Conn.: Greenwood Press, 1978), pp. 123–34.

18. John W. Blassingame, *The Slave Community: Plantation Life in the Antebellum South* (New York: Oxford University Press, 1972); George P. Rawick, *From Sundown to Sunup: The Making of the Black Community* (Westport, Conn.: Greenwood Press, 1972); Herbert G. Gutman, *The Black Family in Slavery and Freedom, 1750–1925* (New York: Pantheon, 1976); Eugene D. Genovese, *Roll, Jordan, Roll* (New York: Random House, 1972); Leslie Howard Owens, *This Species of Property* (New York: Oxford University Press, 1976); Peter H. Wood, *Black Majority: Negroes in Colonial South Carolina from 1670 to the Stono Rebellion* (New York: Alfred A. Knopf, 1974); Sterling Stuckey, "The Black Ethos in Slavery," *Massachusetts Review* 9 (1968), 417–37; Vincent Harding, "Religion and Resistance among Antebellum Negroes, 1800–1860," in August Meier and Elliot Rudwick, eds., *The Making of Black America* (New York: Atheneum, 1969), pp. 179–97.

19. See, for example, Frank Tannenbaum, *Slave and Citizen* (New York: Alfred A. Knopf, 1946), and Patterson, *Slavery and Social Death.*

20. Hare, "What Is Wrong with Slavery?" pp. 106–107.

21. Blassingame, *Slave Testimony.*

22. John Kleinig, *Paternalism* (Totowa, N.J.: Rowman and Allanheld, 1984), and Rolf Sartorius, ed., *Paternalism* (Minneapolis: University of Minnesota Press, 1983).

23. Genovese, *Roll, Jordan, Roll,* and William K. Scarborough, "Slavery: A White Man's Burden," in Harry P. Owens, ed., *Perspectives and Irony in American Slavery* (Jackson: University of Mississippi Press, 1976), pp. 108–109.

24. As early as 1943, commentators responding to U. B. Phillips challenged the idea of a distinctive slave personality. See, e.g., Herbert Aptheker, *American Negro Slave Revolts* (New York: Columbia University Press, 1943).

25. Harvey Natanson, "Locke and Hume: Bearing on the Legal Obligations of the Negro," *Journal of Value Inquiry* 5: 1 (1970), 35–43.

26. See, e.g., Jeffrie G. Murphy, "Forgiveness and Resentment" in Jeffrie G. Murphy and Jean Hampton, *Forgiveness and Mercy* (Cambridge: Cambridge University Press, 1988), chapter 1.

1. Oppression and Slavery

1. Quoted in William Loren Katz, ed., *Five Slave Narratives: A Compendium* (New York: Arno, 1968), p. i.

2. See, for example, George Fitzhugh, *Cannibals All! or Slaves without Masters* (1856; rpt. Cambridge, Mass.: Harvard University Press, 1960); Ulrich B. Phillips, *American Negro Slavery* (New York: D. Appleton, 1918; rpt. Baton Rouge: Louisiana State University Press, 1966); and Eric L. McKitrick, ed.,

Slavery Defended: The Views of the Old South (Englewood Cliffs, N.J.: Prentice-Hall, 1963).

3. Stanley Elkins, *Slavery: A Problem in American Institutional and Intellectual Life* (1959; 3d rev. ed. Chicago: University of Chicago Press, 1976).

4. Orlando Patterson, *Slavery and Social Death* (Cambridge, Mass.: Harvard University Press, 1982); Frank Tannenbaum, *Slave and Citizen* (New York: Alfred A. Knopf, 1946).

5. Kenneth Stampp, *The Peculiar Institution: Slavery in the Antebellum South* (New York, 1956).

6. James Oakes, *Slavery and Freedom* (New York: Alfred A. Knopf, 1990). See also Joe Feagin, "Slavery Unwilling to Die: The Background of Black Oppression in the 1980s," *Journal of Black Studies* 17: 2 (1986), 173–200.

7. See note 1 in the Introduction for a selected listing of slave narratives.

8. Marilyn Frye, for example, takes "to press" to mean to mold, immobilize, or reduce. Marilyn Frye, "Oppression," in *Racism and Sexism: An Integrated Study*, ed. Paula S. Rothenberg (New York: St. Martin's Press, 1988), p. 38.

9. Elkins, *Slavery*, p. 82.

10. John Blassingame, *The Slave Community* (New York: Oxford University Press, 1972), especially chapter 5, "Plantation Stereotypes and Institutional Roles."

11. Ibid., chapter 6, "Plantation Realities."

12. Stampp, *The Peculiar Institution*, p. 10.

13. Ibid., p. 91.

14. Orlando Patterson, *Slavery and Social Death*, p. 8.

15. Historian Peter Parish notes: "Southern slavery does not fit easily even into a work of such prodigious scope." Peter Parish, *Slavery: History and Historians* (New York: Harper and Row, 1989), pp. 112–14.

16. Some commentators have drawn on Patterson's concept of natal alienation for contrasting the effects of American slavery and the Jewish Holocaust on the groups involved. See, for example, Laurence Thomas, "American Slavery and the Holocaust: Their Ideologies Compared," *Public Affairs Quarterly* 5: 2 (1991), 191–207.

17. Sterling Stuckey, *Slave Cultures: Nationalist Theory and the Foundations of Black America* (New York: Oxford University Press, 1987).

18. Frederick Douglass, *The Life and Times of Frederick Douglass* (London: Collier-Macmillan, 1962), pp. 115–26.

19. Linda Brent, *Incidents in the Life of a Slave Girl* (Boston: By the author, 1861).

20. Bertram Wilbur Doyle, *The Etiquette of Race Relations in the South* (New York: Schocken Books, 1971).

21. Quoted in Katz, ed., *Five Slave Narratives: A Compendium*, p. xi.

22. Stampp, *The Peculiar Institution*, p. 430.

23. Oakes, *Slavery and Freedom*, p. 155.

24. Ibid., pp. 155–56.

25. Ibid.

26. Wilbert E. Moore, *American Negro Slavery and Abolition* (New York: Third World Press, 1971), p. 9.

27. Linda Brent, *Incidents in the Life of a Slave Girl* (Boston: By the author, 1861), pp. 117–19.

28. Oakes, *Slavery and Freedom,* p. 156.

29. Ibid., p. 157.

30. Ibid.

31. Quoted in John F. Bayliss, ed., *Black Slave Narratives* (London: Macmillan, 1970), p. 80.

32. Oakes, *Slavery and Freedom,* p. 159.

33. Between 1934 and 1941, as part of the Works Progress Administration workers for the Federal Writers Project interviewed former slaves about their lives in slavery. James Martin's recollections from this project are quoted in James Mellon, ed., *Bullwhip Days: The Slaves Remember* (New York: Weidenfeld and Nicolson, 1988), p. 291.

34. Lunsford Lane, *The Narrative Life of Lunsford Lane* (Boston: privately published, 1842), p. 8.

35. Brent, *Life of a Slave Girl,* p. 57.

36. James W. C. Pennington, *The Fugitive Blacksmith: or, Events in the History of James W. C. Pennington* (2d ed. London: Charles Gilpin, 1849), p. vii.

37. Theodore Brantner Wilson, *The Black Codes of the South* (University, Ala.: University of Alabama Press, 1965), p. 19.

38. L. Mee-yan Cheung-Judge, "The Social Psychological Analysis of Manumission," in Leonie J. Archer, ed., *Slavery and Other Forms of Unfree Labour* (New York: Routledge, 1988), p. 241.

39. Quoted in Wilson, *The Slave Codes,* p. 35.

40. *The Weekly Advocate,* January 14, 1837, p. 2.

41. Maria W. Stewart, "Lecture Delivered at the Franklin Hall, Boston, September 21, 1832," in *Maria W. Stewart: America's First Black Woman Political Writer,* ed. Marilyn Richardson (Bloomington: Indiana University Press, 1987), p. 45.

42. For examples, see Michael P. Johnson and James L. Roark, *Black Masters* (New York: W. W. Norton, 1984).

43. John Hope Franklin, *Racial Equality in America* (Chicago: University of Chicago Press, 1976), p. 34.

44. Solomon Northup, *Twelve Years a Slave: Narrative of Solomon Northup, a Citizen of New York, Kidnapped in Washington City in 1841 and Rescued in January, 1853, from a Cotton Plantation Near Red River in Louisiana* (Buffalo: Derby, Orton and Mulligan, 1853).

45. Waldo Martin, *The Mind of Frederick Douglass* (Chapel Hill: University of North Carolina Press, 1984).

46. Frederick Douglass, "I Denounce the So-Called Emancipation as a Stupendous Fraud," in *The Voice of Black America,* ed. Philips S. Foner (New York: Simon and Schuster, 1972), p. 526.

47. Ibid., p. 521.
48. Ibid., p. 532.
49. Stampp, *The Peculiar Institution.*
50. Feagin, "Slavery Unwilling to Die."
51. Oakes, *Slavery and Freedom,* pp. 198–99; see also Phillips, *American Negro Slavery.*
52. Elmer H. Henderson, "The Federal Government and the Fight for Basic Human Rights," in *Negotiating the Mainstream,* ed. Harry A. Johnson (Chicago: American Library Association, 1978), 141–63.
53. Armstead L. Robinson, "The Difference Freedom Made: The Emancipation of Afro-Americans," in Darlene Clark Hine, ed., *The State of Afro-American History* (Baton Rouge: Louisiana State University Press, 1986), p. 53.

2. Paternalism and Slavery

1. Ulrich B. Phillips, *American Negro Slavery* (New York: D. Appleton, 1918; rpt. Baton Rouge, La.: Louisiana State University Press, 1966); William K. Scarborough, "Slavery: A White Man's Burden," in Harry P. Owens, ed., *Perspectives and Irony in American Slavery* (Jackson: University of Mississippi Press, 1976) pp. 103–36; and Robert Fogel and Stanley Engerman, *Time On the Cross: The Economics of American Negro Slavery* (Boston: Little, Brown, 1974).
2. Kenneth Stampp, *The Peculiar Institution: Slavery in the Antebellum South* (New York, 1956); and John Blassingame, *The Slave Community* (New York: Oxford University Press, 1972).
3. James W. C. Pennington, *The Fugitive Blacksmith: or, Events in the History of James W. C. Pennington* (2d ed., London: Charles Gilpin, 1849), p. iv.
4. Peter Parish, *Slavery: History and Historians* (New York: Harper and Row, 1989), pp. 124–25.
5. Eugene Genovese, *Roll, Jordan, Roll* (New York: Pantheon, 1974), p. 5.
6. Ibid.
7. Scarborough, "Slavery: A White Man's Burden," in Harry P. Owens, ed., *Perspectives and Irony in American Slavery* (Jackson: University of Mississippi Press), pp. 108–109.
8. Genovese, *Roll, Jordan, Roll,* p. 661.
9. For a good description of the "Sambo" personaility, see Stanley M. Elkins, *Slavery* (Chicago: University of Chicago Press, 1976), p. 82.
10. Quoted in William Loren Katz, ed., *Five Slave Narratives: A Compendium* (New York: Arno Press, 1968), p. vi.
11. Stampp, *The Peculiar Institution,* p. 5.
12. I thank Felmon Davis for this possible line of argument.
13. See chapter 1.
14. See, for example, George Fitzhugh, *Cannibals All! or Slaves without Masters* (1856; rpt. Cambridge, Mass.: Harvard University Press, 1960), especially chapter 19.

15. See John Blassingame, *The Slave Community* (New York: Oxford University Press, 1972).

16. Douglass Husak, "Paternalism and Autonomy," *Philosophy and Public Affairs* 10: 1 (1981), 43–46.

17. See Joel Feinberg, "Legal Paternalism," p. 3, and Gerald Dworkin, "Paternalism," in Rolf Sartorius, ed., *Paternalism* (Minneapolis: University of Minnesota Press, 1983), p. 28.

18. Stampp, *The Peculiar Institution,* p. 327.

19. Dworkin, "Paternalism."

20. For a good account of this debate, see Rolf Sartorius, "Paternalistic Grounds for Involuntary Civil Commitment: A Utilitarian Perspective," in Sartorius, *Paternalism,* pp. 95–102.

21. Genovese, *Roll, Jordan, Roll,* p. 5.

22. John Rawls, *A Theory of Justice* (Cambridge, Mass.: Harvard University Press, 1971), pp. 3–4.

23. For a discussion of the medical model, see Allen E. Buchanan, "Medical Paternalism," in Sartorius, *Paternalism,* pp. 61–73.

24. Robert J. Cottrol, "Liberalism and Paternalism: Ideology, Economic Interest and the Business of Slavery," *American Journal of Legal History* 31: 4 (1987), 368.

25. Ibid., p. 364, and G. M. Fredrickson, *The Black Image in the White Mind: The Debate on Afro-American Character and Destiny, 1817–1914* (New York: Harper and Row, 1971), pp. 68–78.

26. Rawls, *Theory of Justice,* and Robert Nozick, *Anarchy, State, and Utopia* (New York: Basic Books, 1974).

27. Darlene Clark Hine, "Lifting the Veil, Shattering the Silence: Black Women's History in Slavery and Freedom" in Darlene Clark Hine, ed. *The State of Afro-American History* (Baton Rouge: Louisiana State University Press, 1986); Angela Davis, *Women, Race, and Class* (New York: Vintage, 1983); Gerder Lerner, ed., *Black Women in White America: A Documentary History* (New York: Pantheon, 1972); Deborah Gray White, *Ar'n't I a Woman? Female Slaves in the Plantation South* (New York: W. W. Norton, 1985); and Paula Giddings, *When and Where I Enter: The Impact of Black Women on Race and Sex in America* (New York: Bantam, 1988).

28. Solomon Northup, *Twelve Years a Slave* (New York: Dover Publications, 1970), pp. 85–86.

3. Resistance and Slavery

1. See, for instance, Herbert Aptheker, *American Negro Slave Revolts* (New York: Alfred A. Knopf, 1943).

2. See Raymond A. Bauer and Alice H. Bauer, "Day to Day Resistance to Slavery," *Journal of Negro History* 27: 4 (1942), 388–419.

3. See George M. Fredrickson and Christopher Lasch, "Resistance to Slavery," in Ann J. Lane, ed., *The Debate Over Slavery* (Urbana: University of Illi-

nois Press, 1971), pp. 223–44 and Lawrence Levine, *Black Culture and Black Consciousness: Afro-American Folk Thought from Slavery to Freedom* (New York, 1977).

4. Linda Brent, *Incidents in the Life of a Slave* (Boston: By the author, 1861) p. 26.

5. Herbert Gutman, *The Black Family in Slavery and Freedom, 1750–1925* (New York: Pantheon, 1976), p. 73.

6. Stanley Elkins, *Slavery: A Problem in American Institutional and Intellectual Life,* (1959; 3d rev. ed. Chicago: University of Chicago Press, 1976), chapter 3.

7. See, for example, Ulrich B. Phillips, *American Negro Slavery* (New York: D. Appleton, 1918; rpt. Baton Rouge: Louisiana State University Press, 1969).

8. See, for example, Kenneth Stampp, *The Peculiar Institution* (New York: Vantage Books, 1956).

9. A good example of the practice of pretending to be sick can be found in the narrative of William Grimes, *The Life of William Grimes* in William Loren Katz, ed., *Five Black Lives* (Middletown, Conn.: Wesleyan University Press, 1971), pp. 81–82.

10. Roger S. Gottlieb, "The Concept of Resistance: Jewish Resistance during the Holocaust," *Social Theory and Practice* 9: 1 (1983), 31–49.

11. Laurence Thomas, "American Slavery and the Holocaust: Their Ideologies Compared," *Public Affairs Quarterly* 5: 2 (1991), 191–207.

12. For accounts of the "Sambo" personality and its role in the slave community, see John W. Blassingame, *The Slave Community: Plantation Life in the Antebellum South* (New York: Oxford University Press, 1972), esp. pp. 200–16; and Orlando Patterson, "Towards a Future That Has No Past: Reflections on the Fate of Blacks in the Americas," *The Public Interest* 27 (1972), 43. For several excellent philosophical discussions of the consequences of the "Sambo" personality on the self-concept, see Thomas E. Hill, Jr., "Servility and Self-Respect," *The Monist* 57: 1 (1973), 87; Laurence Thomas, "Morality and Our Self-Concept," *Journal of Value Inquiry* 12: 4 (1978); and Bernard Boxill, "Self-Respect and Protest, *Philosophy and Public Affairs* 6: 1 (1976).

13. Gottlieb, "The Concept of Resistance," pp. 39–40.

14. See chapter 5 of this volume.

15. Gottlieb, "The Concept of Resistance," pp. 34–47.

16. See William L. Van Deburg, *The Slave Driver: Black Agricultural Labor Supervision in the Antebellum South* (Westport, Conn.: Greenwood Press, 1979).

17. Gottlieb, "The Concept of Resistance," p. 34.

18. Ibid., p. 43.

19. Ibid., p. 45.

20. See Cleveland Sellars (with Robert Terrell), *The River of No Return: Autobiography of a Black Militant and the Life and Death of SNCC* (New York: Morrow, 1973), pp. 46–47.

21. For a good argument in support of the claim that people can intend to

do what they believe to be impossible see Irving Thalberg, "Can One Intend the Impossible?" in *Enigmas of Agency* (New York: Allen and Unwin, 1972).

22. Orlando Patterson, "Towards a Future That Has No Past: Reflections on the Fate of Blacks in the Americas," *The Public Interest* 27 (1972), 43.

23. The play of slave children is an area that might prove extremely useful in spelling out the nature and extent of such behaviors. See, for example, David K. Wiggins, "The Play of Slave Children in the Plantation Communities of the Old South, 1820–1860," *Journal of Sport History* 7: 2 (1980), 21–39.

24. I would like to thank David Benfield, Douglas Husak, Walton Johnson, Brian McLaughlin, Kenneth Monteiro, Irving Thalberg, and members of the Society for the Study of Black Philosophy for their comments and criticisms of earlier drafts of this section.

25. Marilyn Friedman discusses the conditions for a genuine public dialogue in her paper "The Impracticality of Impartiality," *Journal of Philosophy* 86: 11 (1989), 645–56.

26. Donald Davidson, "Actions, Reasons and Causes," *Journal of Philosophy* 60: 23 (1963), 685–700.

27. I thank Laurence Thomas for this example and line of criticism.

28. Aristotle, *Nicomachean Ethics* 1115b7–1116a10.

4. Citizenship and Slavery

1. See, for example, David Donald, *The Politics of Reconstruction* (Baton Rouge: Louisiana State University Press, 1965) and Horace E. Flack, *The Adoption of the Fourteenth Amendment* (Baltimore: Johns Hopkins University Press, 1988).

2. United States Constitution.

3. Quoted in Charles Fairman, *Reconstruction and Reunion 1864–1888: Part One* (New York: Macmillan, 1971), p. 1181.

4. Kwando M. Kinshasa, *Emigration vs. Assimilation* (Jefferson, N.C.: McFarland, 1988).

5. George M. Fredrickson, *The Black Image in the White Mind: The Debate on Afro-American Character and Destiny, 1817–1914* (New York: Harper Torchbooks, 1972), pp. 130–64.

6. Fredrickson, *Black Image,* p. 130.

7. Howard McGary, Jr., "Racial Integration and Racial Separatism: Conceptual Clarifications," in Leonard Harris, ed., *Philosophy Born of Struggle* (Dubuque, Ia.: Kendall/Hunt, 1983), pp. 199–211.

8. I follow here Kinshasa's summary of debates in the black press, in *Emigration vs. Assimilation,* pp. 110–20.

9. Robert Brock, "Morton Downey, Jr., Show," August 18, 1988. Brock also argues for reparations for blacks. The question of reparations has been discussed in the philosophical literature. See, for example, Bernard Boxill, "The Morality of Reparations," *Social Theory and Practice* 2: 1 (1972), 113–22; How-

ard McGary, "Justice and Reparations," *Philosophical Forum* 9: 2/3 (1977–78), 250–63; J. W. Nickle, "Should Reparations Be to Groups or Individuals?" *Analysis* 34: 5 (1973), 154–60.

10. Harvey Natanson, "Locke and Hume: Bearing on the Legal Obligation of the Negro," *Journal of Value Inquiry* 5: 1 (1970), 35–43. While blacks in the Northern part of the United States might have been denied some political protection, for many Southern blacks governmental protection was almost nil. It is these blacks that Natanson must believe are not members of the contract.

11. See, for example, Harry J. Carman and Harold C. Syrett, *A History of the American People* (New York: Alfred A. Knopf, 1975), pp. 114ff.; J. W. Gough, *John Locke's Political Philosophy* (London: Oxford, 1950), p. 103; and Alfred H. Kelly and Winfred A. Harbison, *The American Constitution,* (New York: W. W. Norton, 1963), p. 90.

12. Natanson, "Locke and Hume," p. 35.

13. See, for example, Eric Foner, *Reconstruction: America's Unfinished Revolution 1863–1877* (New York: Harper and Row, 1988), pp. 163–65.

14. This does not mean that there has not been a change in their formal status, but that their real status has not changed. See, for example, Joe Feagin, "Slavery Unwilling to Die: The Background of Black Oppression in the 1980s," *Journal of Black Studies* 17: 2 (1986), 173–200.

15. See, for example, Imari Abubakari Obadele, *Free the Land!* (Washington, D.C.: House of Songhay, 1984).

16. John Locke quoted in Natanson, "Locke and Hume," p. 36.

17. For a discussion of the issue of protection and political obligation, see Bill Lawson, "African-Americans, Crime Victimizations, and Political Obligations," in Diane Shank and David I. Caplan, eds., *To Be a Victim: Encounters with Crime and Injustice* (New York: Plenum, 1991), pp. 141–58.

18. "Reconstruction was a time of hope, the period when the Thirteenth, Fourteenth, and Fifteenth Amendments were adopted, giving Negroes the vote and the promise of equality.

"But campaigns of violence and intimidation accompanied these optimistic expressions of a new age, as the Ku Klux Klan and other secret organizations sought to suppress the emergence into society of the new Negro citizens. Major riots occurred in Memphis, Tennessee, where 46 Negroes were reported killed and 75 wounded, and in the Louisiana centers of Colfax and Coushatta, where more than 100 Negro and white republicans were massacred." *Report of the National Advisory Commission on Civil Disorders* (Washington, D.C.: U.S. Government Printing Office, 1968), p. 98.

19. Natanson, "Locke and Hume," p. 39.

20. Ibid., p. 37.

21. Ibid., p. 39.

22. Ibid.

23. Ibid.

24. Ibid.

25. Stanley M. Elkins, *Slavery: A Problem in American Institutional and Intellectual Life* (Chicago: University of Chicago Press, 1976), pp. 249–50.

26. I. A. Obadele, "The Struggle Is for Land", in Robert Chrisman and Nathan Hare, eds., *Pan-Africanism* (New York: Bobbs-Merrill, 1974), pp. 175–92.

27. Sheldon H. Harris, *Paul Cuffe: Black America and the African Return* (New York: Simon and Schuster, 1972), p. 69.

28. See, for example, Benjamin Quarles, *The Negro in the Civil War* (Boston: Little, Brown, 1953), pp. 132–62.

29. Ibid., p. 157.

30. Elkins, *Slavery;* Foner, *Reconstruction;* John Blassingame, *The Slave Community* (New York: Oxford University Press, 1972); and W. E. B. DuBois, *Black Reconstruction* (1935; rpt. Millwood, N.Y.: Kraus-Thomas, 1963).

31. Franklin, *From Slavery to Freedom,* p. 317.

32. In 1833, the British Empire had attempted to solve its slave problem by the institution of a five-year period of transition called apprenticeship. This plan proved unsuccessful, however, and was terminated before the five years had ended. Complete and immediate emancipation was then adopted. Charles H. Wesley and Patricia W. Romero, *Negro Americans in the Civil War* (New York: Publishers Company, 1967), pp. 114–67.

33. Charles Sumner had proposed establishing the Freedmen's Bureau as a permanent agency with a secretary of cabinet rank—an institutionalization of the nation's responsibility to the freed slaves—but such an idea ran counter to the strong inhibitions against long-term guardianship. Indeed, at the last moment, Congress redefined the bureau's responsibilities so as to include Southern white refugees as well as freedmen, a vast expansion of its authority that aimed to counteract the impression of preferential treatment for blacks. Foner, *Reconstruction,* p. 69.

34. Wesley and Romero, *Negro Americans,* p. 134.

35. See, for example, Horace Mann Bond, *The Education of the Negro in the American Social Order* (New York: Octagon Books, 1966); George R. Bentley, *A History of the Freedmen's Bureau* (Philadelphia: University of Pennsylvania Press, 1955); Henderson H. Donald, *The Negro Freedman* (New York: Henry Schuman, 1952); W. E. B. DuBois, "The Freedmen's Bureau," *Atlantic Monthly* 87 (1901), pp. 354–65; Walter L. Fleming, *Civil War and Reconstruction in Alabama* (New York: Columbia University Press, 1905); Paul S. Pierce, *The Freedmen's Bureau: A Chapter in the History of Reconstruction* (Iowa City: Haskell House, 1904).

36. Milton D. Morris, *The Politics of Black America* (New York: Harper and Row, 1975), pp. 49–118; William A. Russ, "The Negro and White Disfranchisement during Radical Reconstruction," *Journal of Negro History* 19: 2 (1934), 171–92; C. Van Woodward, *Reunion and Reaction: The Compromise of 1877 and the End of Reconstruction* (Boston: Little, Brown, 1951).

37. John Locke, *The Second Treatise on Government,* ed. Thomas P. Peardon (New York: Bobbs-Merrill, 1952), p. 112, sec. 199.

38. Ibid., p. 123, sec. 222.
39. Ibid., p. 111, sec. 198.
40. Sig Synnestvedt, *The White Response to Black Emancipation* (New York: Macmillan, 1972).
41. Locke, *Second Treatise,* p. 123, sec. 221.
42. Ibid., p. 130, sec. 232.
43. Ibid., p. 131, sec. 233.
44. Ibid., p. 123, sec. 222.
45. For a discussion of the development of national citizenship, see Ten Broek, *The Anti-Slavery Origins of the Fourteenth Amendment* (Berkeley: University of California Press, 1951).
46. Locke, *Second Treatise,* p. 138, sec. 242.
47. Ibid., p. 130, sec. 233.
48. See John Rawls, *A Theory of Justice* (Cambridge, Mass.: Harvard University Press, 1971), pp. 46–70; and Larry Thomas, "To a Theory of Justice: An Epilogue," *Philosophical Forum* 6: 2–3 (1975), 244–53.
49. Joseph H. Carens, "Who Belongs? Theoretical and Legal Question about Birthright Citizenship in the United States," *University of Toronto Law Journal* 37: 4 (1987), 413–35.
50. The question of citizenship for blacks was thought to be resolved with the passage of the Fourteenth Amendment. The conferring of citizenship on blacks was first presented in the Civil Rights Act of 1866. Its most important part began: "all persons born in the United States are hereby declared to be citizens of the United States." See Terry Eastland and William J. Bennett, *Counting by Race: Equality from the Founding Fathers to Bakke and Weber* (New York: Basic Books, 1979), p. 61.
51. Carens notes that, for example, Britain and the United States took different views on the question of whether citizenship acquired at birth entailed perpetual allegiance or could be terminated by voluntary expatriation and subsequent naturalization in a new country. This was an important source of conflict between the two countries for much of the nineteenth century. The most common problems arise from the fact that differences in nationality laws leave some people stateless and others with dual citizenship (which sometimes entails conflicting sets of obligations). "Who Belongs?," p. 415.
52. See, for example, P. Weis, *Nationality and Statelessness in International Law* (Westport, Conn.: Hyperion Press, 1956) and Marc Vishniak, "The Legal Status of Stateless Persons," "Jews and the Postwar World" 6 (New York: American Jewish Committee, 1954).
53. Natanson, "Locke and Hume," p. 42.
54. See Bill Lawson, "Crime, Minorities and the Social Contract," *Criminal Justice Ethics* 9: 2 (1990), 16–24.
55. John Rawls, *A Theory of Justice,* pp. 363–94.

5. Moral Discourse and Slavery

1. Justice Bradley quoted in Mortimer J. Adler, ed., *The Negro in American History* (New York: William Benton, 1969), p. 220.

2. Ibid.

3. Ibid., p. 221.

4. Ludwig Wittgenstein, *Philosophical Investigations,* trans. G. E. M. Anscombe (3d ed. New York: Macmillan, 1953), p. 115.

5. See, for example, Mary Vetterling-Braggin, ed., *Sexist Language: A Modern Philosophical Analysis* (Totowa, N.J.: Littlefield, Adams, 1981).

6. Gerald MacCallum, *Political Philosophy* (Englewood Cliffs, N.J.: Prentice-Hall, 1987), p. 157.

7. Winthrop D. Jordon, *White over Black: American Attitudes toward the Negro, 1550–1812* (Chapel Hill: University of North Carolina Press, 1968), parts 4 and 5, especially chapters 11 and 15.

8. *Life and Selected Writings of Thomas Jefferson,* ed. Adrienne Koch and William Peden (Franklin Center, Penn.: Franklin Library, 1982), p. 256.

9. Justice Taney quoted in Wilbert E. Moore, *American Negro Slavery and Abolition* (New York: Third World Press, 1971), p. 91.

10. Milton D. Morris, *The Politics of Black America* (New York: Harper and Row, 1975), p. 82.

11. Sig Synnestvedt, *The White Response to Black Emancipation* (New York: Macmillan, 1972), p. 77.

12. William J. Wilson, *The Truly Disadvantaged* (Chicago: University of Chicago Press, 1987), p. 113.

13. Adrienne Lehrer, *Semantic Fields and Lexical Structure* (London: North-Holland, 1974), p. 16.

14. Ibid., p. 95.

15. Ibid., p. 105.

16. Ibid.

17. Ibid., p. 106.

18. Michael P. Johnson and James L. Roark, *Black Masters: A Free Family of Color in the Old South* (New York: W. W. Norton, 1984), p. xiii.

19. For a discussion of a conceptual gap in the study of the social contract as a motif (in particular between *mutua obligato* and covenant), see Harro Hopfl and Martyn P. Thompson, "The History of Contract as a Motif in Political Thought," *American Historical Review* 84: 4 (1979), 930.

20. John Hope Franklin, *From Slavery to Freedom* (New York: Alfred A. Knopf, 1967), pp. 214–41.

21. Alphonso Pinkney, *Black Americans* (Englewood Cliffs, N.J.: Prentice-Hall, 1987).

22. Wilson notes that "at mid-twentieth century, liberal black and white leaders of the movement for racial equality agreed that the conditions of racial and ethnic minorities could best be improved by an appeal to the conscience

of white Americans to uphold the American creed of egalitarianism and democracy." *The Truly Disadvantaged,* p. 112.
    23. Ibid.
    24. Ibid., p. 113.
    25. William Raspberry quoted in ibid.
    26. Mike W. Martin, *Everyday Morality* (Belmont, Calif.: Wadsworth, 1989), p. 155.
    27. Wilson, *The Truly Disadvantaged,* p. 120.
    28. Bernard Boxill, *Blacks and Social Justice* (Totowa, N.J.: Rowman and Allanheld, 1984), p. 148.
    29. Ibid.
    30. Robert Paul Wolff, "The Concept of Social Injustice," in Fred Dallmayr, ed., *From Contract to Community* (New York: Marcel Dekker, 1978), p. 78; Boxill, *Blacks and Social Justice,* pp. 150–51.
    31. Lisa Newton, "Reverse Discrimination as Unjustified," *Ethics* 83: 4 (1973), 308–12.
    32. Michael Levin, "Is Racial Discrimination Special?" *Journal of Value Inquiry* 15: 3 (1981) 225–34.
    33. Wolff, "Concept of Social Injustice," p. 78.
    34. Robert J. Fogelin, *Understanding Arguments* (New York: Harcourt Brace Jovanovich, 1987), p. 43.
    35. David Green, *Shaping Political Consciousness* (Ithaca, N.Y.: Cornell University Press, 1987), p. 2.
    36. Joel Kupperman, "Character and Ethical Theory," in Peter French, Theodore E. Vehling, Jr., and Howard K. Wettsleen, eds. *Ethical Theory: Character and Virtue,* Midwest Studies in Philosophy 13 (Notre Dame, IN: University of Notre Dame Press, 1988), pp. 115–25.
    37. As the philosopher John Austin noted: "When we examine what we should say when, what words we should use in what situations, we are looking again not merely at words (or 'meanings,' whatever they may be) but also at the realities we use words to sharpen our perception of, though not as the final arbiter of, the phenomena." John L. Austin, "A Plea for Excuses," in J. O. Urmson and G. J. Warnock, eds., *Philosophical Papers* (New York: Oxford University Press, 1979), p. 182.
    38. Farhang Zabeeh, *What Is in a Name?* (The Hague: Martinus Nijhoff, 1968), pp. 66–68.
    39. Haig A. Bosmajian, *The Language of Oppression* (Washington, D.C.: Public Affairs Press, 1974), pp. 33–61.
    40. William Loren Katz, ed., *Five Slave Narratives: A Compendium* (New York: Arno Press, 1968), p. vi.
    41. R. Travis Osborn, Clyde E. Noble and Nathaniel Weyl, *Human Variation: The Biopsychology of Age, Race, and Sex* (New York: Academic Press, 1978), pp. 383–84.
    42. Murray Edelman, *Political Language* (New York: Academic Press, 1977), p. 119.

43. Richard Shenkman, *Legend and Lies: Cherished Myths of American History* (New York: William Morrow, 1988), p. 125.

44. John Austin, "A Plea for Excuses," p. 198.

6. Forgiveness and Slavery

1. William Grimes, "Life of William Grimes," in Arna Bontemps, ed., *Five Black Lives* (Middletown, Conn.: Wesleyan University Press, 1971), pp. 98–99.

2. Albert J. Raboteau, *Slave Religion* (New York: Oxford University Press, 1978), p. 303.

3. See R. S. Downie, "Forgiveness," *Philosophical Quarterly* 15: 59 (1965), 128–34; and Joseph Beatty, "Forgiveness," *American Philosophical Quarterly* 7: 3 (1970): 246–52.

4. For a discussion of the relationship between the religious and the secular conceptions of forgiveness, see Meirlys Lewis, "On Forgiveness," *Philosophical Quarterly* 30: 120 (1980), 236–45; and Anne C. Minas, "God and Forgiveness," *Philosophical Quarterly* 25: 99 (1975), 138–50.

5. Jeffrie G. Murphy, "Forgiveness and Resentment," in Peter A. French, Theodore E. Uehling, Jr., and Howard Wettstein eds., *Midwest Studies,* vol. 7: *Social and Political Philosophy* (Minneapolis: University of Minnesota Press, 1982), p. 504.

6. Ibid., pp. 504, 508.

7. I have benefited greatly on this point from Uma Narayan's unpublished manuscript "Varieties of Forgiveness."

8. Murphy, "Forgiveness and Resentment," p. 508.

9. Ibid., p. 509.

10. Frederick Douglass, *Life and Times of Frederick Douglass* (London: Collier Books, 1962), pp. 115–27.

11. See P. Twambley, "Mercy and Forgiveness," *Analysis* 36: 2 (1976), 89.

12. Downie, "Forgiveness," p. 130.

13. Lawrence Blum, "Compassion," in Robert B. Kruschwitz and Robert C. Roberts, eds., *The Virtues* (Belmont, CA: Wadsworth, 1987), p. 234.

14. Murphy, "Forgiveness and Resentment," p. 504.

15. Ibid., p. 508.

16. Ibid., p. 513.

17. Laurence H. Davis, *A Theory of Action* (Englewood Cliffs, N.J.: Prentice-Hall, 1979), p. 15.

18. Robert Kraut, "Feelings in Context," *Journal of Philosophy* 83: 11 (1986), 647–48.

19. C. G. Montefiore and H. Lowe, *A Rabbinic Anthology* (New York: Schocken Books, 1974), chapter 19, and G. F. Moore, *Judaism* (Cambridge, Mass.: Harvard University Press, 1927–30), vol. 1, chapter 6 and vol. 2, chapter 5.

20. Montefiore and Lowe, *A Rabbinic Anthology.*

21. Thomas Hill, Jr., "Servility and Self-Respect," *The Monist* 57: 1 (1973), 87–104.

22. John Rawls, *A Theory of Justice* (Cambridge, Mass.: Harvard University Press, 1971), pp. 440–46.

23. Laurence Thomas, "Self-Respect: Theory and Practice," in Leonard Harris, ed., *Philosophy Born of Struggle* (Dubuque, Ia.: Kendall/Hunt, 1983), pp. 174–89.

24. Rawls, *A Theory of Justice,* p. 440.

25. Bernard Boxill, "Self-Respect and Protest," in Harris, ed., *Philosophy Born of Struggle,* p. 195.

26. Ibid., p. 196.

27. See, for example, the special issue of *Philosophical Forum* on "Philosophy and the Black Experience": *The Philosophical Forum* 9: 2/3 (1977–78).

28. Jeffrie Murphy and Jean Hampton, *Forgiveness and Mercy* (Cambridge: Cambridge University Press, 1988), p. 89.

29. I am grateful to Mary Gibson, Douglass Husak, Brian McLauglin, Uma Narayan, Laurence Thomas, and members of the philosophy department at the University of Illinois at Chicago for their comments and suggestions on earlier drafts of this chapter. Of course, I bear full responsibility for any errors that remain.

BIBLIOGRAPHY

Adler, Mortimer J., ed. *The Negro in American History.* New York: William Benton, 1969.

Allen, Anita. *Uneasy Access: Privacy for Women in a Free Society.* Totowa, N.J.: Rowan and Littlefield, 1988.

Anderson, James D. "Political and Scholarly Interests in the 'Negro Personality': A Review of *The Slave Community.*" In *Revisiting Blassingame's "The Slave Community,"* edited by Al-Tony Gilmore. Westport, Conn.: Greenwood Press, 1978, pp. 123–34.

Anderson, William J. *Life and Narrative of William J. Anderson; or, Dark Deeds of American Slavery Revealed, Written by Himself.* Chicago: Daily Tribune Book and Job Printing Office, 1854.

Aptheker, Herbert. *American Negro Slave Revolts.* New York: Columbia University Press, 1943.

Austin, John. "A Plea for Excuses." in *Philosophical Papers,* edited by J. O. Urmson and G. J. Warnock. New York: Oxford University Press, 1979.

Ball, Charles. *Slavery in the United States; A Narrative of the Life of Charles Ball, a Black Man, Who Lived Forty Years in Maryland, South Carolina, and Georgia as a Slave.* New York: John S. Taylor, 1837.

Banner, William. *Moral Norms and Moral Order.* Gainesville: University Presses of Florida, 1981.

Bauer, Raymond A., and Alice H. Bauer. "Day to Day Resistance to Slavery." *Journal of Negro History* 27: 4 (1942), 388–419.

Bayliss, John F., ed. *Black Slave Narratives.* London: Macmillan, 1970.

Beatty, Joseph. "Forgiveness." *American Philosophical Quarterly* 7: 3 (1970), 246–52.

Bentley, George R. *A History of the Freedmen's Bureau.* Philadelphia: University of Pennsylvania Press, 1955.

Bibb, Henry. *Narrative of the Life of Henry Bibb, an American Slave, Written by Himself.* New York: By the Author, 1850.

Blassingame, John W. *The Slave Community: Plantation Life in the Antebellum South.* New York: Oxford University Press, 1972.

——. *Slave Testimony.* Baton Rouge: Louisiana State University Press, 1977.

——. "Using the Testimony of Ex-slaves: Approaches and Problems." In *The Slaves' Narrative,* edited by Charles T. Davis and Henry Louis Gates, Jr. Pp. 78–97.

Blum, Lawrence. "Compassion." In *The Virtues,* edited by Robert B. Kruschwitz and Robert C. Roberts. Belmont, Calif.: Wadsworth, 1987, pp. 229–36.

Bond, Horace Mann. *The Education of the Negro in the American Social Order.* New York: Octagon Books, 1966.

Bosmajian, Haig A. *The Language of Oppression.* Washington, D.C.: Public Affairs Press, 1974.

Boxill, Bernard. *Blacks and Social Justice.* Totowa, N.J.: Rowman and Allanheld, 1984.

———. "The Morality of Reparations." *Social Theory and Practice* 11: 2 (1972), 113–22.

———. "The Race-Class Question." In Leonard Harris, ed., *Philosophy Born of Struggle.* Dubuque, Ia.: Kendall/Hunt, 1983, pp. 107–16.

———. "Self-Respect and Protest." *Philosophy and Public Affairs* 6: 1 (1976), 58–69.

Bracey, John H., August Meir, and Elliot Rudwick, eds. *American Slavery: The Question of Resistance.* Belmont, Calif.: Wadsworth, 1971.

Brent, Linda. *Incidents in the Life of a Slave Girl.* Boston: By the author, 1861.

Brewer, James H. *The Confederate Negro.* Durham, N.C.: Duke University Press, 1969.

Brock, Robert. "Morton Downey, Jr., Show." August 18, 1988.

Brown, Isaac. *Case of the Slave Isaac Brown: An Outrage Exposed!* N.p.: n.p., 1847.

Brown, Jane. *Narrative of the Life of Jane Brown and Her Two Children: Related to the Reverend G. W. Offley.* Hartford: Published for G. W. Offley, 1860.

Brown, William Wells. *Narrative of William Wells Brown, a Fugitive Slave, Written by Himself.* Boston: Anti-Slavery Office, 1847.

Buchanan, Allen E. "Medical Paternalism." In *Paternalism,* edited by Rolf Sartorius. Minneapolis: University of Minnesota Press, 1983, pp. 61–81.

Burton, Annie L. *Memories of Childhood's Slavery Days.* Boston: Ross Publishing Company, 1919.

Carens, Joseph H. "Who Belongs? Theoretical and Legal Questions about Birthright Citizenship in the United States." *University of Toronto Law Journal* 37: 4 (1987), 413–35.

Carman, Harry J., and Harold C. Syrett. *A History of the American People.* New York: Alfred A. Knopf, 1975.

Cheung-Judge, L. Mee-yan. "The Social Psychological Analysis of Manumission." In *Slavery and Other Forms of Unfree Labour,* edited by Leonie J. Archer. New York: Routledge, 1988, pp. 239–50.

Cooper, Anna J. *A Voice from the South.* 1892; rpt. New York: Negro Universities Press, 1969.

Cottrol, Robert J. "Liberalism and Paternalism: Ideology, Economic Interest and the Business of Slavery." *American Journal of Legal History* 31: 4 (1987), 359–73.

Craft, William. *Running a Thousand Miles for Freedom: or, the Escape of William and Ellen Craft from Slavery.* London: W. Tweedie, 1860.

Davidson, Donald. "Actions, Reasons and Causes." *Journal of Philosophy* 60: 23 (1963), 685–700.

Davis, Angela. *Women, Race, and Class.* New York: Vintage, 1983.

Davis, Charles T., and Henry Louis Gates, Jr., eds. *The Slaves' Narrative.* New York: Oxford University Press, 1985.

Davis, David Brion. *The Problem of Slavery in Western Culture.* New York: Oxford University Press, 1966.

Davis, Laurence H. *A Theory of Action.* Englewood Cliffs, N.J.: Prentice-Hall, 1979.

Dinah. *The Story of Dinah, as Related to John Hawkins Simpson, after Her Escape from the Horrors of the Virginia Slave Trade, to London.* London: A. W. Bennett, 1863.

Donald, David. *The Politics of Reconstruction.* Baton Rouge, La.: Louisiana State University Press, 1965.

Donald, Henderson H. *The Negro Freedman.* New York: Henry Schuman, 1952.

Douglass, Frederick. "The Claims of the Negro Ethnologically Considered." In *The Voice of Black America,* edited by Philip S. Foner. New York: Simon and Schuster, 1972, pp. 144–64.

——. "I Denounce the So-Called Emancipation as a Stupendous Fraud." In *The Voice of Black America,* edited by Philip S. Foner. New York: Simon and Schuster, 1972, pp. 520–36.

——. *Life and Times of Frederick Douglass.* 1892; rpt. London: Collier Books, 1962.

——. *Narrative Life of Frederick Douglass, an American Slave. Written by Himself.* Boston: Boston Anti-Slavery Office, 1845.

Downie, R. S. "Forgiveness." *Philosophical Quarterly* 15: 59 (1965), 128–34.

Doyle, Bertram Wilbur. *The Etiquette of Race Relations in the South.* New York: Schocken Books, 1971.

Du Bois, W. E. B. *Black Reconstruction.* 1935; rpt. Millwood, N.Y.: Kraus-Thomas, 1963.

——. "The Freedmen's Bureau." *Atlantic Monthly* 87 (March 1901), 354–65.

——. *The Soul of Black Folks.* 1903; rpt. New York: New American Library, 1969.

Dworkin, Gerald. "Paternalism." In *Paternalism,* edited by Rolf Sartorius. Minneapolis: University of Minnesota Press, 1983, pp. 19–34.

Eastland, Terry, and William J. Bennett. *Counting by Race: Equality from the Founding Fathers to Bakke and Weber.* New York: Basic Books, 1979.

Edelman, Murray. *Political Language.* New York: Academic Press, 1977.

Eldridge, Elleanor. *Memoirs of Elleanor Eldridge.* Providence: B. T. Albro, 1847.

Elkins, Stanley M. *Slavery: A Problem in American Institutional and Intellectual Life.* 3d rev. ed. Chicago: University of Chicago Press, 1976.

Escott, Paul D. *Slavery Remembered.* Chapel Hill: University of North Carolina Press, 1979.

Fairman, Charles. *History of the Supreme Court of the United States,* vol. 6, *Reconstruction and Reunion 1864–1888, Part One.* New York: Macmillan, 1971.

Feagin, Joe. "Slavery Unwilling to Die: The Background of Black Oppression in the 1980s." *Journal of Black Studies* 17: 2 (1986), 173–200.

Feinberg, Joel. "Legal Paternalism." In *Paternalism*, edited by Rolf Sartorius. Minneapolis: University of Minnesota Press, 1983, pp. 3–18.

——. *Social Philosophy*. Englewood Cliffs, N.J.: Prentice-Hall, 1973.

Finkelman, Paul, ed. *Articles on American Slavery*, vol. 9, *Women and the Family in a Slave Society*. New York: Garland, 1989.

Fitzhugh, George. *Cannibals All! or Slaves without Masters*. 1856; rpt. Cambridge, Mass.: Harvard University Press, 1960.

Flack, Horace E. *The Adoption of the Fourteenth Amendment*. Baltimore: Johns Hopkins University Press, 1908.

Fleming, Walter L. *Civil War and Reconstruction in Alabama*. New York: Columbia University Press, 1905.

Fogel, Robert William. *Without Consent or Contract*. New York: W. W. Norton, 1989.

Fogel, Robert, and Stanley Engerman. *Time on the Cross: The Economics of American Negro Slavery*. Boston: Little, Brown, 1974.

Fogelin, Robert J. *Understanding Arguments*. New York: Harcourt Brace Jovanovich, 1987.

Foner, Eric. *Reconstruction: America's Unfinished Revolution 1863–1877*. New York: Harper and Row, 1988.

Foner, Philip S., ed. *The Voice of Black America*. New York: Simon and Schuster, 1972.

Franklin, John Hope. *From Slavery to Freedom*. 3d ed. New York: Alfred A. Knopf, 1967.

——. *Racial Equality in America*. Chicago: University of Chicago Press, 1976.

Fredrickson, George M. *The Arrogance of Race*. Middletown, Conn.: Wesleyan University Press, 1988.

——. *The Black Image in the White Mind: The Debate on Afro-American Character and Destiny, 1817–1914*. New York: Harper and Row, 1971.

Fredrickson, George M., and Christopher Lasch. "Resistance to Slavery." In *The Debate over Slavery*, edited by Ann J. Lane. Urbana: University of Illinois Press, 1971, pp. 223–44.

Friedman, Marilyn. "The Impracticality of Impartiality." *Journal of Philosophy* 86: 11 (1989), 645–56.

Frye, Marilyn. "Oppression." In *Racism and Sexism: An Integrated Study*, edited by Paula S. Rothenberg. New York: St. Martin's Press, 1988, pp. 37–41.

Garnet, Henry Highland. "An Address to the Slaves of the United States of America." In *The Ideological Origins of Black Nationalism*, edited by Sterling Stuckey. Boston: Beacon Press, 1972, pp. 165–73.

Gaspar, David B. *Bondsmen and Rebels*. Baltimore: Johns Hopkins University Press, 1985.

Genovese, Eugene D. *Roll, Jordan, Roll*. New York: Random House, 1972.

Giddings, Paula. *When and Where I Enter: The Impact of Black Women on Race and Sex in America*. New York: Bantam, 1988.

Gilmore, Al-Tony, ed. *Revisiting Blassingame's "The Slave Community."* Westport, Conn.: Greenwood Press, 1978.

Goldberg, David Theo, ed. *Anatomy of Racism.* Minneapolis: University of Minnesota Press, 1991.

Gottlieb, Roger S. "The Concept of Resistance: Jewish Resistance during the Holocaust." *Social Theory and Practice* 9: 1 (1983), 31–49.

Gough, J. W. *Locke's Political Philosophy.* London: Oxford University Press, 1950.

Green, David. *Shaping Political Consciousness.* Ithaca, N.Y.: Cornell University Press, 1987.

Gutman, Herbert G. *The Black Family in Slavery and Freedom, 1750–1925.* New York: Pantheon, 1976.

Harding, Vincent. "Religion and Resistance among Antebellum Negroes, 1800–1860." In *The Making of Black America,* edited by August Meier and Elliot Rudwick. New York: Atheneum, 1969, pp. 179–97.

Hare, R. M. "What Is Wrong with Slavery?" *Philosophy and Public Affairs* 8: 2 (1979), 103–21.

Harris, Leonard, ed. Philosophy Born of Struggle. Dubuque, IA: Kendall/Hunt, 1983.

Harris, Sheldon H. *Paul Cuffe: Black America and the African Return.* New York: Simon and Schuster, 1972.

Haynes, Robert V., ed. *Blacks in White America before 1865.* New York: David McKay, 1975.

Henderson, Elmer H. "The Federal Government and the Fight for Basic Human Rights." In *Negotiating the Mainstream,* edited by Harry A. Johnson. Chicago: American Library Association, 1978, pp. 141–63.

Henson, Josiah. *Truth Stranger Than Fiction: Father Henson's Story of His Own Life.* Boston: John P. Jewett, 1858.

Hill, Thomas E., Jr. "Servility and Self-Respect." *The Monist* 57: 1 (1973), 87–104.

Hine, Darlene Clark, ed. *The State of Afro-American History.* Baton Rouge: Louisiana State University Press, 1986.

Hoetink, Harmannus. *Slavery and Race Relations in the Americas.* New York: Harper and Row, 1973.

Hopfl, Harro, and Martyn P. Thompson. "The History of Contract as a Motif in Political Thought." *American Historical Review* 84: 4 (1979), 919–44.

Huggins, Nathan Irvin. *Black Odyssey.* New York: Pantheon, 1977.

Husak, Douglass. "Paternalism and Autonomy." *Philosophy and Public Affairs* 10: 1 (1981), 27–46.

Jacob, Paul, Saul Landau, and Eve Pell, eds. *To Serve the Devil.* New York: Vantage, 1971.

Johnson, Michael P., and James L. Roark. *Black Masters: A Free Family of Color in the Old South.* New York: W. W. Norton, 1984.

Jones, Jacqueline. *Labor of Love, Labor of Sorrow: Black Women, Work and the Family from Slavery to the Present.* New York: Basic Books, 1985.

Jordan, Winthrop D. *White over Black: American Attitudes toward the Negro, 1550–1812.* Chapel Hill: University of North Carolina Press, 1968.

Katz, William Loren, ed. *Five Slave Narratives: A Compendium.* New York: Arno, 1968.

Keckley, Elizabeth. *Behind the Scenes by Elizabeth Keckley, Formerly a Slave, but More Recently Modiste, and Friend to Mrs. Abraham Lincoln: or, Thirty Years a Slave, and Four Years in the White House.* New York: G. W. Carlton, 1868.

Kelly, Alfred H. and Winfred A. Harbison. *The American Constitution.* New York: W. W. Norton, 1963.

Kinshasa, Kwando M. *Emigration vs. Assimilation.* Jefferson, N.C.: McFarland, 1988.

Kleinig, John. *Paternalism.* Totowa, N.J.: Rowman and Allanheld, 1984.

Kraut, Robert. "Feelings in Context." *Journal of Philosophy* 83: 11 (1986), 542–652.

Kupperman, Joel. "Character and Ethical Theory." In *Ethical Theory,* edited by Peter A. French et al. Midwest Studies in Philosophy 13. Notre Dame, IN: University of Notre Dame Press, 1988, pp. 115–25.

Lane, Ann. *The Debate over Slavery: Stanley Elkins and His Critics.* Urbana: University of Illinois Press, 1971.

Lawson, Bill. "African-Americans, Crime Victimizations, and Political Obligations." In *To Be a Victim: Encounters with Crime and Injustice,* edited by Diane Shank and David I. Caplan. New York: Plenum, 1991, pp. 141–58.

———. "Crime, Minorities and the Social Contract." *Criminal Justice Ethics* 9: 2 (1990), 16–24.

———. "Individuals and Groups in the American Democracy." *Logos* 6 (1985), 105–15.

———. "Locke and the Legal Obligations of Black America." *Public Affairs Quarterly* 3: 3 (1989), 49–63.

———. "Politically Oppressed Citizens." *Journal of Value Inquiry* 25: 4 (1991), 335–38.

———. *The Underclass Question.* Philadelphia: Temple University Press, 1992.

Lehrer, Adrienne. *Semantic Fields and Lexical Structure.* London: North-Holland, 1974.

Lerner, Gerda, ed. *Black Women in White America: A Documentary History.* New York: Pantheon, 1972.

Levin, Michael. "Is Racial Discrimination Special?" *Journal of Value Inquiry* 15: 3 (1981), 225–34.

Lewis, Meirlys. "On Forgiveness." *Philosophical Quarterly* 30: 120 (1980), 236–45.

Locke, John. *The Second Treatise on Government.* Edited by Thomas P. Peardon. New York: Bobbs-Merrill, 1952.

MacCallum, Gerald. *Political Philosophy.* Englewood Cliffs, N.J.: Prentice-Hall, 1987.

Magdol, Edward. *A Right to the Land.* Westport, Conn.: Greenwood Press, 1977.

Marshall, T. H. *Class, Citizenship, and Social Development.* Garden City, N.Y.: Doubleday, 1964.

Martin, Mike W. *Everyday Morality.* Belmont, Calif.: Wadsworth, 1989.

McDade, Jessie, and Carl Lesnor, eds. "Philosophy and the Black Experience." *Philosophical Forum* 9: 2–3 (1977–78).

McGary, Howard, Jr. "The Concept of Resistance: Black Resistance during Slavery." In *Freedom, Equality and Social Change: Problems in Social Philosophy Today,* edited by Yeager Hudson and James Sterba. Lewiston, N.Y.: Edwin Mellen Press, 1989, pp. 280–90.

——. "Forgiveness." *American Philosophical Quarterly* 26: 4 (1989): 343–51.

——. "Justice and Preparations." *Philosophical Forum* 9: 2–3 (1977–78), 250–63.

——. "The Moral Status of Groups." In *Encyclopedia of Ethics,* edited by Lawrence C. Becker and Charlotte B. Becker. New York: Garland, 1992, 422–25.

——. "Morality and Collective Liability." *Journal of Value Inquiry* 7: 2 (1984), 129–37.

——. "Racial Integration and Racial Separatism: Conceptual Clarification." In *Philosophy Born of Struggle,* edited by Leonard Harris. Dubuque, Ia.: Kendall/Hunt, 1983, pp. 199–211.

——. "Reparations, Self-Respect and Public Policy." 1984, revised and reprinted in *Ethical Theory and Society: Historical Texts and Contemporary Readings,* edited by David Goldberg. Holt, Rinehart and Winston, 1989, pp. 280–90.

——. "South Africa: The Morality of Divestment." *Philosophical Forum* 18: 2–3 (1987), 203–12.

McKitrick, Eric L. *Slavery Defended: The Views of the Old South.* Englewood Cliffs, N.J.: Prentice-Hall, 1963.

Meier, August, and Elliot Rudwick, eds. *The Making of Black America.* New York: Atheneum, 1969.

Mellon, James, ed. *Bullwhip Days: The Slaves Remember.* New York: Weidenfeld and Nicolson, 1988.

Mellon, Matthew T., ed. *Early American Views on Negro Slavery.* 1834, rpt. New York: Bergman, 1969.

Mill, J. S. *On Liberty.* Edited by Currin V. Shields. New York: Bobbs-Merrill, 1956.

Minas, Anne C. "God and Forgiveness." *Philosophical Quarterly* 25: 99 (1975), 138–50.

Montefiore, C. G., and H. Lowe. *A Rabbinic Anthology.* New York: Schocken Books, 1974.

Moore, G. F. *Judaism.* 2 vols. Cambridge, Mass.: Harvard University Press, 1927–30.

Moore, Wilbert E. *American Negro Slavery and Abolition.* New York: Third World Press, 1971.

Morgan, James C. *Slavery in the United States: Four Views.* Jefferson, N.C.: McFarland, 1985.

Morris, Milton D. *The Politics of Black America.* New York: Harper and Row, 1975.

Murphy, Jeffrie G. "Forgiveness and Resentment." In *Forgiveness and Mercy,* by

Jeffrie G. Murphy and Jean Hampton. Cambridge: Cambridge University Press, 1988, pp. 14–34.

———. "Forgiveness and Resentment." In *Social and Political Philosophy*, edited by Peter A. French et al. Midwest Studies 7. Minneapolis: University of Minnesota Press, 1982, pp. 503–16.

Murphy, Jeffrie, and Jean Hampton. *Forgiveness and Mercy*. Cambridge: Cambridge University Press, 1988.

Natanson, Harvey. "Locke and Hume: Bearing on the Legal Obligations of the Negro." *Journal of Value Inquiry* 5: 1 (1970), 35–43.

Newby, I. A. *Jim Crow's Defense*. Baton Rouge: Louisiana State University Press, 1965.

Newton, James, and Ronald L. Lewis, eds. *The Other Slaves*. Boston: G. K. Hall, 1978.

Newton, Lisa. "Reverse Discrimination as Unjustified." *Ethics* 83: 4 (1973), 308–12.

Nickle, J. W. "Discrimination and Morally Relevant Characteristics." *Analysis* 32: 4 (1972), 113–14.

———. "Should Reparations Be to Groups or Individuals?" *Analysis* 34: 5 (1973), 154–60.

Northup, Solomon. *Twelve Years a Slave: Narrative of Solomon Northup, a Citizen of New York, Kidnapped in Washington City in 1841 and Rescued in January, 1853, from a Cotton Plantation Near Red River in Louisiana*. Buffalo: Derby, Orton and Mulligan, 1853.

Nozick, Robert. *Anarchy, State, and Utopia*. New York: Basic Books, 1974.

Oakes, James. *Slavery and Freedom*. New York: Alfred A. Knopf, 1990.

Obadele, I. A. *Free the Land!* Washington, D.C.: House of Songhay, 1984.

———. "The Struggle Is for Land." In *Pan-Africanism*, edited by Robert Chrisman and Nathan Hare. New York: Bobbs-Merrill, 1974, pp. 175–92.

Osborn, R. Travis, Clyde E. Noble, and Nathaniel Weyl, eds. *Human Variation: The Biopsychology of Age, Race, and Sex*. New York: Academic Press, 1978.

Osofsky, Gilbert, ed. *Puttin' On Ole Massa*. New York: Harper and Row, 1969.

Owens, Harry P., ed. *Perspectives and Irony in American Slavery*. Jackson: University of Mississippi Press, 1976.

Owens, Leslie Howard. *This Species of Property*. New York: Oxford University Press, 1976.

Parish, Peter. *Slavery: History and Historians*. New York: Harper and Row, 1989.

Patterson, Orlando. *Slavery and Social Death*. Cambridge, Mass.: Harvard University Press, 1982.

———. "Towards a Future That Has No Past: Reflections on the Fate of Blacks in America." *The Public Interest* 27 (1972), 25–62.

Pennington, James W. C. *The Fugitive Blacksmith: or, Events in the History of James W. C. Pennington*. 2d ed. London: Charles Gilpin, 1849.

Phillips, Ulrich Bonnell. *American Negro Slavery: A Survey of the Supply, Employment and Control of Negro Labor as Determined by the Plantation Regime*. 1918; rpt. Baton Rouge: Louisiana State University Press, 1969.

Pierce, Paul S. *The Freedmen's Bureau: A Chapter in the History of Reconstruction.* Iowa City: Haskell House, 1904.

Quarles, Benjamin. *The Negro in the Civil War.* Boston: Little, Brown, 1953.

Raboteau, Albert J. *Slave Religion.* New York: Oxford University Press, 1978.

Rawick, George P. *From Sundown to Sunup: The Making of the Black Community.* Westport, Conn.: Greenwood, 1972.

Rawls, John. *A Theory of Justice.* Cambridge, Mass.: Harvard University Press, 1971.

Redding, Saunders. *They Came in Chains.* Philadelphia: J. B. Lippincott, 1950.

Report of the National Advisory Commission on Civil Rights. Washington, D.C.: Government Printing Office, 1968.

Richardson, Marilyn, ed. *Maria W. Stewart, America's First Black Woman Political Writer.* Bloomington: Indiana University Press, 1987.

Roberts, Ralph. "A Slave's Story." *Putnam's Monthly* 9 (June 1857), 614–20.

Robinson, Armstead L. "The Difference Freedom Made: The Emancipation of Afro-Americans." In *The State of Afro-American History,* edited by Darlene Clark Hine. Baton Rouge: Louisiana State University Press, 1986, pp. 51–76.

Roper, Moses. *A Narrative of the Adventure and Escape of Moses Roper from American Slavery,* with a preface by T. Price. 1840; rpt. New York: Negro Universities Press, 1970.

Russ, William A. "The Negro and White Disfranchisement during Radical Reconstruction." *Journal of Negro History* 19: 2 (1934), 171–92.

Sartorius, Rolf. "Paternalistic Grounds for Involuntary Civil Commitment: A Utilitarian Perspective." In *Paternalism,* edited by Rolf Sartorius, pp. 95–102.

Sartorius, Rolf, ed. *Paternalism.* Minneapolis: University of Minnesota Press, 1983.

Scarborough, William K. "Slavery: A White Man's Burden." In *Perspectives and Irony in American Slavery,* edited by Harry P. Owens. Jackson: University of Mississippi Press, 1976, pp. 103–36.

Sellars, Cleveland, with Robert Terrell. *The River of No Return: Autobiography of a Black Militant and the Life and Death of SNCC.* New York: Morrow, 1973.

Shenkman, Richard. *Legend and Lies: Cherished Myths of American History.* New York: William Morrow, 1988.

Stampp, Kenneth M. *The Peculiar Institution: Slavery in the Antebellum South.* New York: Random House, 1956.

Starling, Marion Wilson. *The Slave Narrative: Its Place in American History.* Boston: G. K. Hall, 1981.

Stepto, Robert B. "Distrust of the Reader in Afro-American Narratives." In *Reconstructing American Literary History,* edited by Sacvan Bercovitch. Cambridge, Mass.: Harvard University Press, 1986, pp. 300–22.

Stewart, Maria W. *Maria W. Stewart: America's First Black Woman Political Writer.* Edited by Marilyn Richardson. Bloomington: Indiana University Press, 1987.

Storing, Herbert J., ed. *What Country Have I?* New York: St. Martin's Press, 1970.

138   Bibliography

Stuckey, Sterling. "The Black Ethos in Slavery." *Massachusetts Review* 9 (Summer 1968), 417–37.

———. *Slave Cultures: Nationalist Theory and the Foundations of Black America.* New York: Oxford University Press, 1987.

Synnestvedt, Sig. *The White Response to Black Emancipation.* New York: Macmillan, 1972.

Tannenbaum, Frank. *Slave and Citizen.* New York: Alfred A. Knopf, 1946.

Ten Broek, Jacobus. *The Anti-Slavery Origins of the Fourteenth Amendment.* Berkeley: University of California Press, 1951.

Thalberg, Irving. *Enigmas of Agency.* New York: George Allen and Unwin, 1972.

Thomas, Laurence. "American Slavery and the Holocaust: Their Ideologies Compared." *Public Affairs Quarterly* 5: 2 (1991), 191–207.

———. *Living Morally.* Philadelphia: Temple University Press, 1989.

———. "Morality and Our Self-Concept." *Journal of Value Inquiry* 12: 4 (1978), 258–68.

———. "Self-Respect: Theory and Practice." In *Philosophy Born of Struggle: Anthology of Afro-American Philosophy from 1917,* edited by Leonard Harris. Dubuque, Ia.: Kendall/Hunt, 1983, pp. 174–89.

———. "To a Theory of Justice: An Epilogue." *Philosophical Forum* 6: 2–3 (1975), 244–53.

Truth, Sojourner. *Narrative of Sojourner Truth, a Northern Slave, Emancipated from Bodily Servitude by the State of New York, in 1828.* Boston: By the author, 1853.

Twambley, P. "Mercy and Forgiveness." *Analysis* 36: 2 (1976), 84–90.

Van Deburg, William L. *The Slave Driver: Black Agricultural Labor Supervision in the Antebellum South.* Westport, Conn.: Greenwood Press, 1979.

———. *Slavery and Race in American Popular Culture.* Madison: University of Wisconsin Press, 1984.

Vander Zander, James W. *American Minority Relations.* New York: Ronald Press, 1966.

Vetterling-Braggin, Mary, ed. *Sexist Language: A Modern Philosophical Analysis.* Totowa, N.J.: Littlefield, Adams, 1981.

Vishniak, Marc. "The Legal Status of Stateless Persons." Pamphlet Series "Jews and the Post-War World" 6. New York: American Jewish Committee, 1954.

Walzer, Michael. *Obligations.* New York: Clarion Books, 1972.

Watson, R. L. *The Slave Question.* Hanover: Wesleyan University Press, 1990.

Weekly Advocate. January 14, 1837, p. 2.

Weis, P. *Nationality and Statelessness in International Law.* Westport, Conn.: Hyperion Press, 1956.

Wesley, Charles H., and Patricia W. Romero. *Negro Americans in the Civil War.* New York: Publishers Company, 1967.

West, Cornel. *Prophesy Deliverance!* Philadelphia: Westminster Press, 1982.

Westermann, William Linn. "Between Slavery and Freedom." *American Historical Review* 50: 2 (1945), 213–27.

White, Deborah Gray. *Ar'n't I a Woman?* New York: W. W. Norton, 1985.

Wiggins, David K. "The Play of Slave Children in the Plantation Communities of the Old South, 1820–1860." *Journal of Sport History* 7: 2 (1980), 21–39.

Wilson, Theodore Brantner. *The Black Codes of the South.* University, Ala.: University of Alabama Press, 1965.

Wilson, William J. *The Truly Disadvantaged.* Chicago: University of Chicago Press, 1987.

Wittgenstein, Ludwig. *Philosophical Investigations.* Translated by G. E. M. Anscombe. 3d ed. New York: Macmillan, 1953.

Wolff, Robert Paul. "The Concept of Social Injustice." In *From Contract to Community,* edited by Fred R. Dallmayr. New York: Marcel Dekker, 1978, pp. 65–79.

Wood, Peter H. *Black Majority: Negroes in Colonial South Carolina from 1670 to the Stono Rebellion.* New York: Alfred A. Knopf, 1974.

Woodward, C. Vann. *Origins of the New South.* Baton Rouge: Louisiana State University Press, 1951.

———. *Reunion and Reaction: The Compromise of 1877 and the End of Reconstruction.* Boston: Little, Brown, 1951.

———. *The Strange Career of Jim Crow.* New York: Oxford University Press, 1955.

Zabeeh, Farhang. *What Is in a Name?* The Hague: Martinus Nijhoff, 1968.

INDEX

Abolitionism: liberalism and rationalizations of slavery, 30

Abortion: influence of language on social policy, 86

Accountability: forgiveness and blame, 99

Actions: morality and forgiveness, 100-102

Affirmative action: moral discourse and slavery experience, 82-85

Agents, moral: defined, xxv; forgiveness and actions, 101

Alienation: oppression and slavery, 3-4

Analytical philosophy: as approach to study of slave narratives, xvii; powerlessness and concepts of oppression and forgiveness, xviii-xix; concept of resistance, 38. *See also* Philosophy

Apartheid: language of moral discourse, 85

Apprenticeship: British Empire and transition from slave system, 123n.32

Authenticity: debate on reliability of slave narratives, xx

Autobiography. *See* Slave narratives

Autonomy: paternalistic explanations of slavery, 29; slavery and political status of blacks after emancipation, 62

Beliefs: defining acts of resistance in terms of, 40-41; concept of unconscious resistance, 42-43; tactics of resistance and sincerity of, 44-45; alternative account of resistance, 48-54

Beneficent institution: belief in slavery as, 21, 22

Benevolent dictator/citizen model: paternalistic accounts of slavery, 28-29

Black liberation movement: beliefs of victims about oppression, 51

Blacks: debate on impact of slavery on political and social status, xxiv-xxv; oppression of freedmen in antebellum period, 9-12; present-day and oppression, 13; failure of government to protect after emancipation, 13-15, 59-60, 64, 75, 122n.10; beliefs in inferiority of as justification for slavery, 23-24; citizenship and slavery, 55-70; social and political history of and lexical gaps in moral/political vocabulary, 78, 89; language and governmental policy, 78-82; language and affirmative action, 82-85; language and understanding of slavery experience, 87-89; self-respect as crucial theme in writings of contemporary, 110-11

Blame: and forgiveness, 99-100

Bradley, Justice Joseph P.: slavery and moral discourse after emancipation, 71-72, 73, 86

Brent, Linda: cruel treatment of female slaves, 5; concept of *partus sequitur ventrem,* 7; attitudes of southern women regarding slaves, 9; slave women and acts of resistance, 35

British Empire: apprenticeship and transition from slavery, 123n.32

Brutality: scholarly debate on slavery, xxv. *See also* Cruelty

Cartwright, Dr. Samuel: apologists for slavery and paternalism, 20-21

Census: language and social status of free blacks in antebellum South, 77-78

Chattels: blacks as property and distinctive character of American slavery, 8-9

Children: government and institution of slavery, 6-7; parent/child model and paternalistic accounts of slavery, 25-26; sale of away from slave mothers, 32-33; intentions and acts of resistance, 47; government and paternalistic position toward blacks and citizenship, 61

Christianity: paternalistic accounts of slavery, 27-28; slave religion and contradiction between slavery and, 91-92; for-

BILL E. LAWSON is Associate Professor of Philosophy at the University of Delaware. His research has focused on political obligations and political oppression, and his work has appeared in numerous philosophical journals. He is the editor and a contributor to *The Underclass Question*.

HOWARD MCGARY is Professor of Philosophy at Rutgers University. He has published widely in African-American philosophy and social philosophy.